Two Hundred Days

Two Hundred Days

My Time as Commander of Operation Removal of Chemical Agents from Syria, 2013-2014

By Torben Mikkelsen, Rear Admiral,
Admiral Danish Fleet and Chief of Navy Command

and

Søren Nørby, PhD, Historical Consultant to
the Royal Danish Navy, Institute for Strategy and
Warstudies, Royal Danish Defence College

University of Southern Denmark Studies in History and Social Sciences Vol. 626
ISBN: 978-87-408-3421-5
Printed by Specialtrykkeriet Arco

For more information about Torben Mikkelsen, see the Appendix.
For more information about Søren Nørby, see www.noerby.net

This book has been published with the support from:
DFDS A/S
A.P. Møller og Hustru Chastine Mc-Kinney Møllers Fond til almene Formaal
Navalteam Denmark
Royal Danish Defence College

Distribution in the United States and Canada:
Independet Publishers Group
www.ipgbook.com

Distribution in the Unite Kingdom:
Gazelle Books
www.gazellebookserices.co.uk

University Press of Southern Denmark
Campusvej 55
DK-5230 Odense M

www.universitypress.dk

Contents

Preface

This book tells an unusual story, namely the story of how former Syrian President Bashar al-Assad's chemical weapons were collected and removed from Syria in the midst of the civil war that had haunted the country since the spring of 2011. In international parlance, this effort is known as Operation RECSYR (Removal of Chemical Agents from Syria). The Syrian regime had amassed a large stockpile of chemical agents, some of which were used in operations in August 2013. Precisely the deployment in August 2013 brought international pressure on the Syrian regime to hand over its chemical weapons for destruction.

The international community managed to persuade President al-Assad to agree to this, and during Operation RECSYR more than 1,300 tons of chemical warfare agents were removed from Syria. The regime of al-Assad thus lost a potential instrument for further terrorisation of the by then sorely tried Syrian population, and we prevented the weapons from falling into the hands of terrorist organisations such as the Islamic State or al-Qaeda.

The RECSYR force with Danish L17 Esbern Snare *in the lead. In the left-hand side of the photo is the Norwegian frigate F313* Helge Ingstad, *and to the right the British frigate F236* Montrose. *20 February 2014.*

Due to my service in the Royal Danish Navy, I had been appointed commander of the naval force tasked with collecting and removing the chemical weapons and agents from Syria. The interesting and not least challenging aspect of this job was to balance the large number of actors, including the United Nations (UN), the Organization for the Prohibition of Chemical Weapons (OPCW) and American, British, Chinese, Russian and, to a minor extent, Syrian interests, while at the same time solving the task together with these actors. In this large strategic puzzle, Denmark merely constituted a small piece, but that said, it is important to remember that even the smallest piece can play a pivotal role, because without it the puzzle will never be complete.

There is nothing unusual about a cargo ship collecting a number of 20-foot containers in a port, just as there is nothing controversial about warships escorting cargo ships and protecting them from potential threats from sea or air. But when the international community through joint efforts manage to remove chemical weapons from Syria within less than a year from decision to completion, while the country was in the throes of a violent civil war, mind you, this feat is nothing short of remarkable. Also unusual is the fact that it was possible to do so even though the superpowers were not in agreement. Their disagreement in particular concerned Russia's actions in Ukraine with the annexation of the Crimea in February-March 2014. Last, but not least, it was remarkable that the operation was not headed by one of the large countries, but by the Danish contribution.

In this book, I share my experiences in connection with Operation RECSYR with the reader. In a way, it is a classic seaman's tale about sailors – tough men and women – who venture into the world to solve an important task. But the book is also a contribution to the history of the Syrian civil war, which has greatly affected developments in the Middle East, as well as political developments in both Europe and Denmark. Last, but not least, it constitutes an important part of the history of Denmark's and the Danish Navy's role in preserving the world order established after the dissolution of the Soviet Union in 1991. Operation RECSYR thus could not have taken place during the Cold War from 1945-1991, and the book is therefore a practical example of the new scope created for Danish foreign policy by this process.

The text is mainly based on the day-to-day journal I kept throughout the operation. The purpose of the journal was three-fold: It helped me keep track of the many events; it served as letters of a sort to my family back home; and finally, previous service had taught me that documenting your decisions can be a good idea. The entries were either written in brief snatches, often during the day whenever my work allowed, or as one coherent text at night, immediately after I had turned in.

Seeing as we are dealing with a journal here, some of the entries are characterised by the events of the day – moments of joy, frustration or irritation. Therefore, some of the entries may offend readers who possess knowledge that was not available to me at the tactical level or at the time. Nevertheless, they are recordings of events as I saw them at the time in question. All in all, the journal is an opportunity to gain an insight into my thoughts as the tactical commander on the scene.

As the journal was written for my own pleasure, it has been necessary to adjust some of the text slightly to ensure that it makes sense to readers who were not there, or who do not work for the Danish Defence. The book therefore alternates between journal entries and transcriptions hereof. At the same time, my account has been placed in the wider context of my and the Danish Navy's efforts in connection with Operation RECSYR, with which Naval Historian Søren Nørby has kindly helped me.

The book also contains a series of short stories affecting both those who were there and their relatives back home. However, the book is an account of Operation RECSYR seen from my position as commander of a multinational naval force. And from that position things may look different than from other positions on board *Esbern Snare*, *Ark Futura* or Norwegian *Helge Ingstad* and *Taiko*. It is therefore not unlikely that an account by one of the crew members on the abovementioned ships would have included elements not mentioned here. However, I am sure that the principal lines of such a story would have been the same, as would their pride in having taken part in such a successful mission.

RECSYR sleeve tag graphically illustrating the path of the toxic gas away from Syria. Worn with pride by those who participated in the operation.

I hope that some of the aspects of the operation described here – not least the deliberations I had to undertake as tactical commander in order to stay abreast of the strategic situation – may be instructive to others in the Danish Defence, to relatives of deployed crews and to the crew members themselves. Similarly, I am inclined to think that it might provide strategic-level decision makers with knowledge that may prove beneficial in connection with similar operations in the future.

Torben Mikkelsen
Hornbæk 2019

***

The Royal Danish Navy. From defence of the Baltic to the Horn of Africa, 1989-2014

Founded in 1510, the Royal Danish Navy (*Søværnet*) is one of the oldest navies in Europe. Until the British bombardment of the Danish capital of Copenhagen and the subsequent raid on the entire Danish Navy in 1807, the Danish Navy was also one of the world's larger navies. The Danish Navy thus builds on a long history, and simply put: without the Danish Navy, there would be no Denmark.

During the last 25 years or so, however, the Danish Navy has changed dramatically. When the Berlin Wall fell in 1989, the Danish Navy consisted of approx. 50 warships, covering the full spectrum from submarines over minelayers and fast attack craft to frigates. Today the fleet has no submarines, no fast attack craft and no dedicated minelayers, and its personnel have been reduced from 5,600 in 1986 to approx. 2,500 in 2014. At the same time, a small number of new ships have been commissioned, and even though the fleet today consists of only five dedicated warships, they – the three frigates of the Iver Huitfeldt class and two support ships of the Absalon class – are the largest, most powerful and most versatile ships that the Danish Navy has ever had at its disposal.

At the same time, the Navy went through this transition, its focus shifted from Danish waters and the Baltic to the high seas. The Navy became a much-used tool for the Danish Government and its new "activist foreign policy". The basic idea behind the activist foreign policy is that Denmark is affected by the globalized world around it, and if the Danish Government wants to maintain peace and stability in Europe, then it can be necessary to intervene in conflicts far from what during the Cold War was called Denmark's neighbouring area.

During the anti-piracy operation off the Horn of Africa, the Danish Navy was involved in combat for the first time since the war against Prussia in 1864. Here a pirate mother ship is blown up following a battle with the support ship Esbern Snare *in 2011.*

Also relevant to the Danish Navy is the fact that approximately 10 % of the world's merchant shipping is carried by Danish-flagged or Danish-owned ships. Maritime security problems such as piracy therefore have a direct impact on the Danish economy, despite the fact that it takes place thousands of miles away.

The Navy's effort to subdue the pirates at the Horn of Africa has claimed many resources. But Denmark being a maritime nation, it was a job that needed to be done. Here the Danish support ship Esbern Snare *meets the world's largest container ship, the Danish-owned* Mærsk Mc-Kinney Møller *of the Triple E-class, at the Horn of Africa in 2014.*

With the Navy's transition to international engagement, the Naval Home Guard has taken over a large part of the daily maritime surveillance, rescue service and environmental monitoring in the Danish waters. The Naval Home Guard is mainly staffed by volunteer personnel, who all approach the task with the professionalism that is needed to operate safely at sea. (P.S. Lynge)

Mission

The Navy's mission statement is to protect Danish interests from the sea – with force if necessary. The Navy is tasked with enforcing Danish sovereignty in home waters and at the same time providing sea rescue and environmental control when needed. In this task, the Navy is assisted by the Naval Home Guard, which operates 30 small vessels in Danish waters.

The Danish Navy is also tasked with patrolling the waters around the Faeroese Islands and Greenland. The ships here are responsible for maintaining a Recognized Surface and Air Picture of the Kingdom's EEZ, which includes fishery inspection, enforcing the Danish/Greenlandic/Faeroese sovereignty and sea rescue in the vast area.

The ocean patrol vessel F359 Vædderen *in Greenland.*

Organisation

The Danish Navy's ships are organised into two squadrons. The 1st Squadron based in Frederikshavn is tasked with deploying ships and crews for the tasks in Danish, Faeroese and Greenlandic waters. This squadron also handles the Navy's environmental ships, the Royal Yacht, the Coastal Rescue Service, and the Surveying Service.

The 2nd Squadron based in Korsør is responsible for the ships deployed on international operations, e.g. off Africa. At Korsør is also the Naval Surveillance Centre, which keeps an eye on the maritime traffic in Danish waters from eleven land-based centres.

Ademiral Danish Fleet HQ is co-located withe the trung and Air Force Staffs at Airstation Karup in Jutland. In case of large operations and with the daily responsibility for training the ships' complements in sea going operations, the Navy in 2001 created a new command called the Danish Task Group. The Task Group, which consists of a core staff of about 20 personnel, can be tasked with a wide range of assignments, from crisis management, peacekeeping and peace-making operations to the conduct of outright war. The Danish Task Group is a deployable capacity and can lead international maritime operations on a Task Group level from any platform at sea or ashore, which it has done on several occasions, e.g. during the anti-piracy-operations off Africa.

Naval Base Frederikshavn – the Danish Navy has two naval bases, one at Korsør by the Great Belt and one at Frederikshavn near the tip of Jutland. Both were built during the 1960s, partially with NATO funding, and have fairly modern facilities.

The Navy has one school, which runs seven subordinate, specialised centres (technical training, diving, tactics, weapons, maritime safety and firefighting, basic training and Petty Officers school. The school staff is based in Frederikshavn.

The Naval Academy has been organisationally transferred to a subordinate unit, together with the Army and Air Force Academies, under the Danish Defence College in Copenhagen. The Academy is still situated at the old naval base Holmen in Copenhagen, which was the Navy's main base from 1690-1993. At Holmen is also the home of the Naval Band, the Centre for Diver Training and the Centre for Technical Training.

The Danish Navy 2019

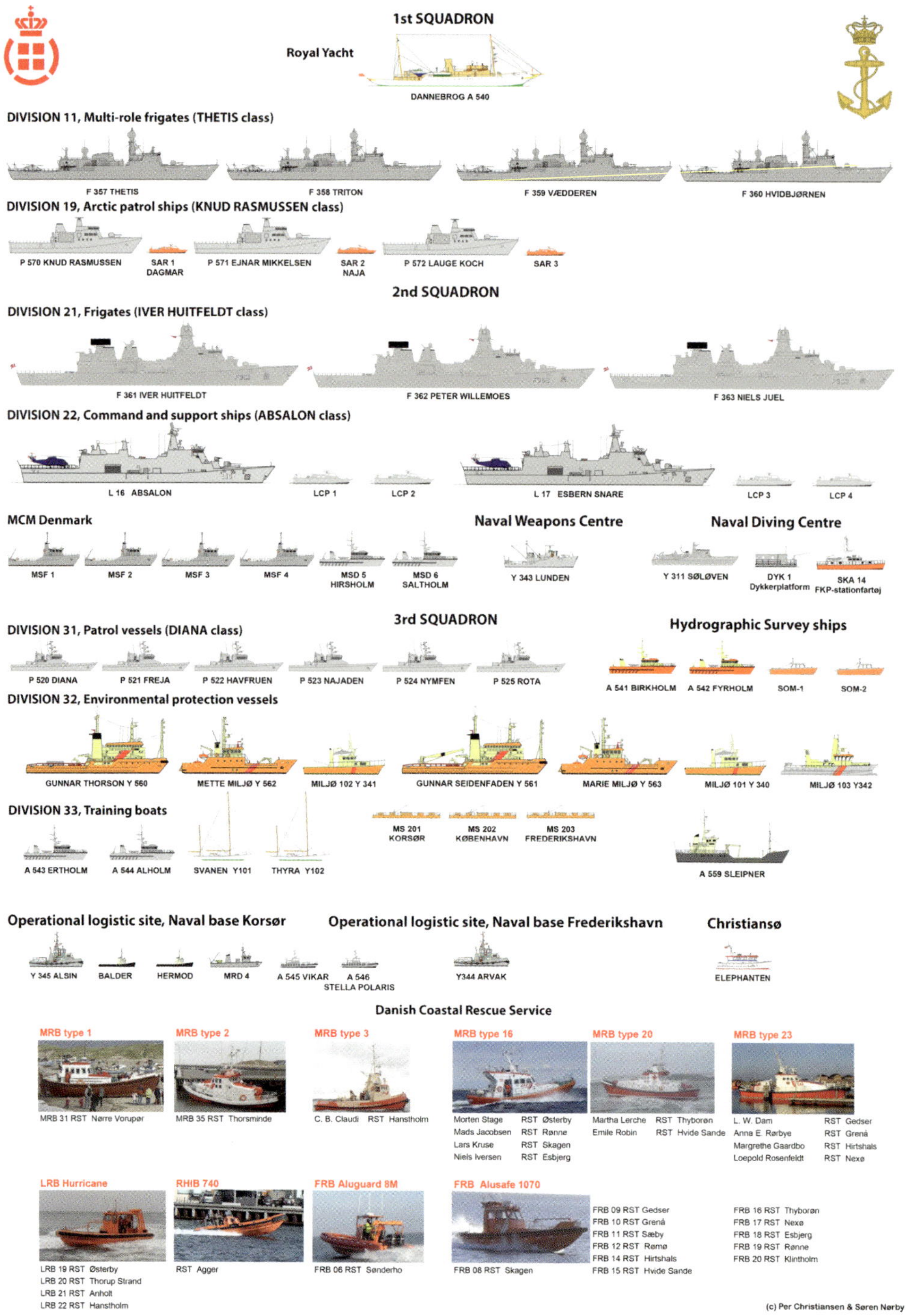

Type	Class	Name	Pennant number	Date of commissioning
Frigate	IVER HUITFELDT	*Iver Huitfeldt*	F361	21 January 2011
-	-	*Peter Willemoes*	F362	22 June 2011
-	-	*Niels Juel*	F363	7 November 2011
Command and Support Ship (Reclassed as a frigate in 2020)	ABSALON	*Absalon*	L16 (Changed to F341 in 2020)	19 October 2004
-	-	*Esbern Snare*	L17 (Changed to F342 in 2020)	18 April 2005
Ocean patrol ship	THETIS	*Thetis*	F357	1 July 1991
-	-	*Triton*	F358	2 December 1991
-	-	*Vædderen*	F359	9 June 1992
-	-	*Hvidbjørnen*	F360	30 November 1992
Ocean patrol vessel	KNUD RASMUSSEN	*Knud Rasmussen*	P570	18 February 2008
-	-	*Ejnar Mikkelsen*	P571	16 January 2009
-	-	*Lauge Koch*	P572	Under construction
-	AGDLEK	*Tulugaq*	Y388	26 June 1979
Patrol vessel	DIANA	*Diana*	P520	12 December 2007
-	-	*Freja*	P521	30 May 2008
-	-	*Havfruen*	P522	25 September 2008
-	-	*Najaden*	P523	11 December 2008
-	-	*Nymfen*	P524	4 May 2009
-	-	*Rota*	P525	12 December 2009
Mine sweeper	MSF	*Unnamed*	MSF1, MSF2, MSF3, MSF4	1998-1999
-	HOLM	*Hirsholm*	MSD5	29 June 2007
-	-	*Saltholm*	MSD6	28 March 2008
Environmental protection ships	SUPPLY	*Gunnar Thorson*	A560	1 January 1996
-	-	*Gunnar Seidenfaden*	A561	1 January 1996
Environmental protection vessel	SEATRUCK	*Mette Miljø*	A562	1 January 1996
-	-	*Marie Miljø*	A563	1 January 1996
Surveying vessels	HOLM	*Birkholm*	A541	27 January 2006
-	-	*Fyrholm*	A542	21 December 2006
Royal yacht		*Dannebrog*	A540	26 May 1932
Training ship	SVANEN	*Svanen*	Y101	31 August 1960
-	-	*Thyra*	Y102	25 May 1961
-	HOLM	*Ertholm*	A543	5 August 2006
-	-	*Alholm*	A544	2 July 2007
Transport ship		*Sleipner*	A559	18 July 1986

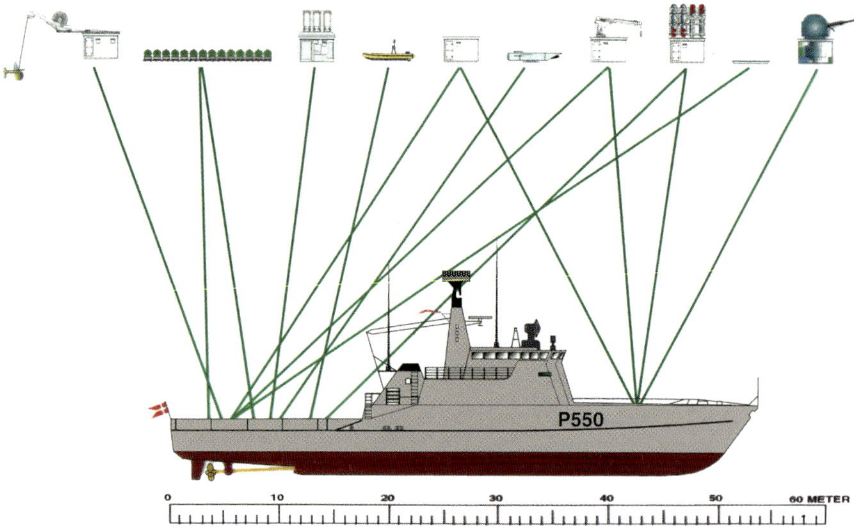

A central design feature of almost all major Danish warships is the StanFlex container system. Using this system, where weapons, cranes/davits, rubber dinghies or other equipment is placed in containers, the ships are able to change role quite rapidly.

The Danish Navy acquired its first helicopter in 1962. Eight Alouette helicopters served the Danish Navy, mostly from the ocean patrol vessels as organic helicopters, around Greenland and the Faeroe Islands until 1982, when they were replaced with the Westland Lynx. The Lynx served the Danish Navy with distinction – from the Arctic to the Horn of Africa, but in 2012 the Danish parliament decided to allocate funds for the replacement of the Lynx with the American MH-60R Seahawk, the first of which arrived in 2017. The acquisition of the new and larger helicopter has necessitated a complete overhaul of the hangar deck on board the ocean patrol vessels of the Thetis class.

The Danish Navy of today is small yet operates some of the most potent and long-range vessels ever seen in its history. Here the frigate Iver Huitfeldt *is photographed meeting the Norwegian frigate* Fridtjof Nansen *during Operation Ocean Shield off Africa in January 2013. (T. Dyhr)*

FOST

Having spent many man-hours and resources in a low-intensity fight against pirates during the 2000s, the Navy has in recent years taken a number of steps to raise its professional competency level. Both the frigates of the Iver Huitfeldt class and *Absalon* and *Esbern Snare* have participated – and passed – the challenging training at the British Navy's "Fleet Operational Sea Training" (FOST).

At the same time, a number of crews have been trained at the German Navy's "Damage Control Training Centre" (DCTC) at Neustadt. Here they have learned important lessons about damage control at sea, which has led to a number of changes in ship organisation.

***

The Syrian Civil War

The story of Operation RECSYR actually began on 18 December 2010 in a public square in the Tunisian town of Sidi-Bouzid. Here, 26-year-old Mohamed Bouazizi, an unemployed academic, chose to set himself on fire after police had confiscated the vegetable cart that constituted his livelihood. Bouazizi's suicide triggered events that would result in the resignation of Tunisia's long-time dictator, Ben Ali, in January 2011. Like falling dominos, the riots soon spread to the neighbouring countries. The so-called Arab Spring became a reality, and in February 2011, Egypt's long-time dictator, Hosni Mubarak, too, was overthrown. The

The Arab Spring also struck Libya, which saw an uprising against the country's long-time dictator, Muammar al-Gaddafi, in February 2011. The Libyan security forces suppressed the rebels violently. To prevent what looked like the onset of a genocide, the UN chose to impose a no-fly zone above Libya in March 2011. Danish F-16s participated in the operation, which over the course of the summer turned into an actual air campaign against Gaddafi's military forces. In the period of March-October 2011, Danish F-16s thus dropped 923 bombs on military installations and forces loyal to Gaddafi. On 20 October, Muammar al-Gaddafi was captured by the rebel forces and executed, which signalled an end to incidents of major fighting in Libya.

'spring' then spread to Iran, Jordan, Libya, Bahrain – and on 15 March 2011, it reached Syria.

In Syria, the 'spring' began as peaceful protests against President Bashar al-Assad. He had run the country since 2000, having taken over from his father, Hafez al-Assad, who had ruled as dictator of Syria since 1970. Those Syrians who, through peaceful demonstrations, expressed a wish for improvement, and perhaps even the introduction of a form of democracy, were met with violence by al-Assad's forces. Syrian security forces were deployed, resulting in the killing of several protestors and wounding of hundreds of others. This did not put an end to the riots, however, which spread to several Syrian cities, and soon the country was embroiled in a civil war.

Syria, a relatively young nation, was the product of the Ottoman Empire's dissolution after the First World War, when French and British diplomats Francois Georges Picot and Mark Sykes, respectively, negotiated a great-power agreement, thereby creating Syria. The lines they drew on the map did not take into consideration the local population's ethnicity or their aspirations (un.org).

Bashar al-Assad (b. 1965) has ruled as the autocratic president of Syria since 2000, when he succeeded his father, Hafez al-Assad. Originally, it was Bashar al-Assad's older brother who had been groomed to take over the leadership of the country, but when his older brother was killed in a traffic accident in 1994, Bashar al-Assad had to give up his ophthalmology studies in London and return to Syria. (Ritzau/Scanpix)

The civil war developed, as these things often do, into a complex conflict with various actors and even more stakeholders. The al-Assad regime was challenged by an amalgam of rebel groups and militias – some records speak of more than 1,000 different small and large groups – some of which wanted to replace the al-Assad regime with an Islamic caliphate, while others wanted a more Western-inspired government. Their only unifying factor was their opposition to al-Assad. A series of countries chose more or less openly to support either the rebels or the al-Assad regime, and while Saudi Arabia, the US, Great Britain, Turkey and Qatar supported the rebels, Iran and Russia backed al-Assad. In addition, non-state terrorist organisations such as Hezbollah, the Workers' Party of Kurdistan (PKK), Islamic State (ISIL) and al-Qaeda also played a role.

The war has swayed to and fro and is still ongoing at the time of writing. At times, the al-Assad regime seemed to be at the breaking point, but in recent years the president, backed by Iran and Russia, has seen battlefield successes. As is always the case in conflicts like these, the real losers are the civilian population. At the time of writing, more than 400,000 Syrians have been killed, and approx. two million have been wounded, while about 10 million out of the approx. 22 million people who lived in Syria in 2011 have either been internally displaced or fled the country. At the same time, the average age of the Syrian population has dropped from 70 years in 2011 to 55 in 2015.

Map of the Eastern Mediterranean Sea with its historical centres. In 1971 the Soviet Union acquired a small naval base at the Syrian port of Tartus. Following the dissolution of the Soviet Union in 1991, the base was transferred to Russia. This base is immensely important today as Russia's only naval strongpoint in the area. In the winter of 2012, the base was expanded, now able to accommodate up to 11 warships, including nuclear-powered submarines, and in 2013 the Russian Navy re-established its Fifth Mediterranean Squadron, based in Tartus, and tasked with safeguarding Russian interests in the Mediterranean.

The Red Line

The Syrian civil war soon became a problem in the neighbouring countries, causing large flows of refugees to enter Lebanon and Turkey, in particular. Yet to the rest of the world, the civil war was just one of several ongoing conflicts, and the US and the West did not have enough at stake to intervene directly with their own forces. To put it bluntly, the civil war was crowded out by the many other wars and conflicts in newspaper headlines during those years. Up until the summer of 2013, the Syrian civil war was therefore more or less ignored. This changed at the end of August, when reports from Syria described the use of poison gasses in hostilities close to the Syrian capital of Damascus. According to these reports, one or more successive attacks had cost hundreds of mainly civilian lives.

It is never easy to examine such episodes while the fighting is still ongoing, but the international organisation, Doctors Without Borders, who were present in the area, estimated that at least 355 persons had been killed in the attack or attacks. Shortly afterwards, the US Government announced that according to its surveys, the poison gas used during the fighting was most likely sarin, which attacks the human nervous system. Sarin is considered one of the world's most dangerous nerve gasses and has been characterised by the UN as a weapon of mass destruction. Use hereof is therefore illegal under several conventions, including the 1997 UN Chemical Weapons Convention.

It was the first time since 1988, when Iraqi dictator Saddam Hussein had used chemical weapons against the Kurdish minority in Iraq, that such weapons had been used in war or conflict, which therefore attracted considerable international attention. The Syrian Government immediately blamed the country's rebel forces, who just as quickly retorted that Bashar al-Assad was responsible.

In Europe, poison gasses were used during The first World War, when both German and Allied Forces, especially on the Western Front, made use of various types of poison gasses. Since The first World War, poison gas has only been used in the war between Iraq and Iran in 1980-88, as well as internally in Iraq by dictator Saddam Hussein against the Kurds in 1988. In both cases, the use of poison gas was strongly condemned by the international community, which nevertheless did not take steps to prevent the use of chemical weapons from happening again. Before August 2011 there had been rumours of chemical weapons use in the Syrian civil war, but the photos published in August 2013 left no doubt as to the cause of death of the many civilians. The exact number of victims in the attacks on 21 August is still a moot point; some sources argue that the poison gasses killed as many as 1,400 people. As is evident from the photo above, several of the victims were children. (Ritzau/Scanpix)

The International Community's Reaction

Even though the Syrian regime had never confirmed or denied possessing poison gas, it was general knowledge that the regime since the 1970s had been in possession of considerable amounts of poison gas. Credible sources thus estimated that the Syrian stockpile of poison gas exceeded 1,000 tons, which made it the world's third largest, only exceeded by Russia and the US. The Syrian stockpile of chemical weapons, which had been amassed to counterbalance Israel's nuclear weapons, also included, in addition to sarin, more potent gasses such as mustard gas and VX nerve agent.

Due to the fighting, though, it was uncertain whether the country's entire stockpile of poison gas was still controlled by the regime. However, the US Government believed it had evidence that President al-Assad's forces had been responsible for the poison gas attack on 21 August 2013. US President Barack H. Obama had, as early as August 2012, warned the Syrian president that using or transferring chemical weapons would be considered a violation of a 'red line'. Such a violation would prompt a US military reaction. In the days following the gas attack, Obama, among other things, deployed four, later followed by another two, US warships to the waters off Syria. From here, they were able to attack targets ashore with long-range Tomahawk missiles, and the general expectation was that a US-led attack was in the offing. The prestige of the US president was at stake, but Obama failed to secure the support of the Republican-controlled Congress for a military attack on Syria, and without said support he refused to deploy US forces in a civil war which at the time seemed without end in sight.

A contributing factor to this lack of support was the fact that an attempt to eliminate the Syrian stockpile of chemical weapons by military means would require a very extensive operation. The Syrian forces loyal to the government commanded an extensive air defence system that would have to be eliminated before the US could hit the sites of the chemical agent stockpiles. History has shown that such air raids would hardly have succeeded in destroying all the chemical substances. Therefore, to ensure that the chemical agents were either destroyed or

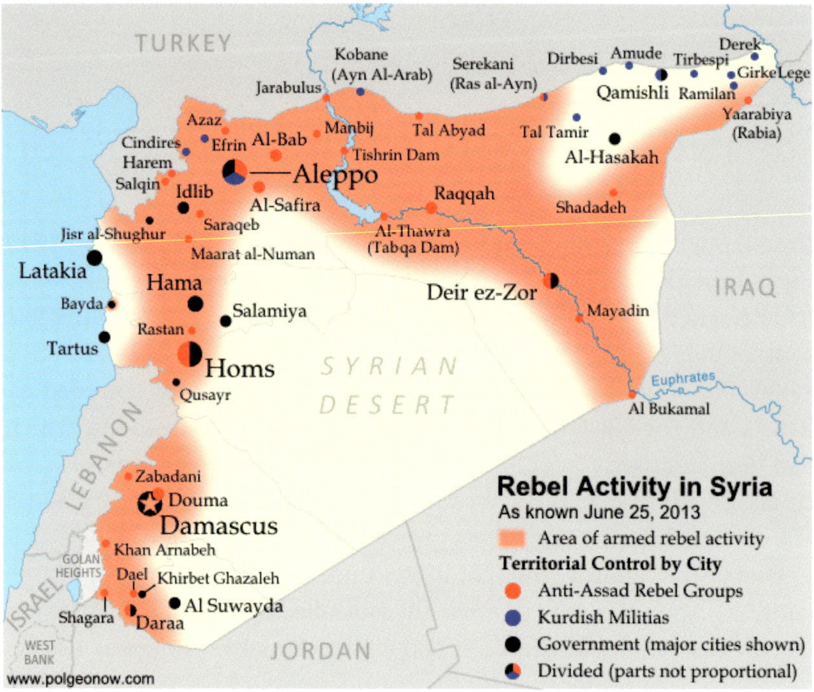

In the summer of 2013, al-Assad's forces were under massive pressure, and many observers of the civil war believed that it was only a matter of time before al-Assad would suffer defeat. This made the Syrian regime desperate, leading it to use poison gas against the rebel forces. (www.polgeonow.com)

removed, the Americans would have to launch a large number of air and missile strikes, or even commit ground forces.

In the British Parliament, the Conservative Government also lost a vote on whether or not to make military forces available for an attack on al-Assad's forces. Following the many Western losses in Iraq, in particular, and experiences from Libya in 2011-12, where the removal of dictator Muammar Gaddafi had left the country in a state of anarchy, neither Western politicians nor their populations were ready for a new war in the Middle East.

Instead, the initiative was passed to Russia, which as one of President al-Assad's few allies on the international scene, wanted to avoid an attack on the Syrian regime. A US attack against the part of the Syrian armed forces loyal to al-Assad would in all probability cause the president to lose his grip on power – which is what had happened in Libya in

2012. To avoid this, the Russian foreign minister, Sergey Lavrov, suggested on 11 September 2013 that the Syrian chemical weapon stockpile be transferred into international custody and subsequently destroyed.

Denmark Becomes Involved

In the weeks that followed, the Russian proposal met with support from both Syria, Iran, China and the US. On 27 September 2013, the UN Security Council thus unanimously passed Resolution 2118, which gave Syria approx. nine months to destroy its stockpile of chemical weapons. The deadline was 30 June 2014. If Syria were to fail in meeting this deadline, the Resolution, based on Article VII of the Charter of the United Nations, allowed for US forces to attack Syria.

Responsibility for managing the threat of chemical weapons currently rests with the international, intergovernmental Organization for the Prohibition of Chemical Weapons (OPCW). It was established in 1997 to enforce an international convention prohibiting the production, stockpiling, trade, transfer and use of chemical weapons, and thanks to the efforts of the OPCW, among others, 78 per cent of the world's known stockpiles of chemical weapons were destroyed in the period 1997-2013.

In 2013, the OPCW, which is based in The Hague in the Netherlands, counted 189 member states. Among the few countries that had so far refrained from signing the OPCW charter was Syria, but a key element in the new agreement between the UN and the Syrian Government was that the country would have to sign the charter. The Syrian Government thus agreed to destroy its own ability to produce chemical weapons and to transfer its stockpile of already produced chemical war agents for destruction.

By signing the agreement, al-Assad did not just ward off a US military attack. He also managed to appear to the international community as the leader of Syria, even though large parts of the country were in fact beyond his control at this point in time. To al-Assad, this therefore constituted a win-win situation, to use a modern-day expression, and losing his stockpile of chemical weapons was, all things considered, an acceptable price to pay.

On the basis of Resolution 2118, a joint UN-OPCW group was established to coordinate the further effort to destroy Syria's chemical

Sigrid Kaag visiting Esbern Snare *in 2014.*

weapons. On 13 October the task was placed in the hands of Dutch diplomat Sigrid Kaag, and at the same time the OPCW set up a base in Cyprus and a Joint Mission in Latakia, Syria, from where the operation would be coordinated and run. The UN would contribute with logistics, security, administration and communications, while the OPCW would provide the technical expertise and maintain dialogue with the Syrian Government.

During the course of October, OPCW staff inspected the 23 known Syrian sites for chemical weapons production. They were subsequently destroyed by Syrian military personnel, under the supervision of as many as 100 OPCW personnel. The country's stockpile of grenades and bombs meant to deliver the chemical weapons to the battlefield suffered a similar fate. On 31 October the OPCW announced that all production sites and all ammunition had now been destroyed. Now 'all' that remained was to eliminate the up to 1,300 tons of chemical agents held in a number of locations in western Syria. Due to safety and environmental considerations, the agents could not be destroyed onsite but had to be transported out of the country to be destroyed safely elsewhere.

The chemical agents were grouped as first- and second-priority agents, depending on the extent to which they had been prepared and were ready for warfare use. The first-priority agents included the warfare agent mustard gas and the main component for the nerve gas sarin, while the second-priority agents comprised various types of poisonous chemicals, mainly alcohols and acids, which can be used in the production of chemical weapons. The second-priority agents were therefore classified as standard dangerous goods, large amounts of which are transported across the oceans every day.

No one volunteered to receive the chemical agents, and it was therefore decided that the first-priority agents would undergo hydrolysation. For this purpose, the American ship *Cape Ray* was equipped with two mobile hydrolysis systems, which by way of fission, could transform the chemical agents into 'standard' dangerous goods similar to the agents normally destroyed in chemical factories. The second-priority agents would not be destroyed on board *Cape Ray* but brought to a port in Italy from which they would be transported to a destruction facility.

The agreement was that Syrian forces would carry the chemical substances to a Syrian port, from where they would be loaded onto a cargo ship, which would then transport them to a destruction facility. However, such a cargo ship, filled with chemical substances, would constitute a tempting target to al-Assad's adversaries or terrorist organisations. A military escort was therefore necessary to protect both the ship and its cargo.

Cape Ray *is a cargo ship belonging to the US Navy, and it is normally used to ship provisions from the US to various American naval bases around the world. In connection with Operation RECSYR,* Cape Ray *was equipped with two hydrolyses systems capable of hydrolysing the most dangerous chemical agents. In total,* Cape Ray *hydrolysed approx. 530 tons of chemical agents during Operation RECSYR. (www.navsource.org)*

Considering its 500-year history, the Royal Danish Navy was not unaccustomed to the type of assignment with which it was tasked in connection with Operation RECSYR. In the 1700s and 1800s, it was not unusual for Danish warships to escort Danish-Norwegian cargo ships, just as deployed Danish naval officers have previously handled diplomatic duties for Danish allies and enemies. The above painting shows ship of the line Indfødsretten *(in front and centre) escorting the Danish China ships* Kongen af Danmark *and* Disko *as well as the Swedish China ship* Finland *safely home from the Cape of Good Hope in 1781. (The Museum of National History at Frederiksborg Castle)*

As both the US and British Governments had threatened to attack Syria in the summer of 2013, the Syrian Government refused to let them be responsible for protecting the cargo ships tasked with disposing of the country's chemical weapons. Similarly, the US and Great Britain – and the rest of the world for that matter – did not trust the Russians to do the job impartially, as the Russian Government had sided with the al-Assad regime. It was therefore necessary to find a country that had warships suited for the task, but which had no part in the power struggle in Syria. At the end of October, Denmark thus received an unofficial enquiry from the US Government, asking if the Danish Navy would be interested either in contributing to the operation with a warship and a cargo ship or in running the entire operation. The Norwegian Government received a similar enquiry. The Danish Government quickly replied that it was ready both to make a warship and a cargo ship available to the operation and to take on the overall responsibility for the entire operation. The Americans accepted.

An Operation Comes into Being

In November 2013, the Danish Government informed the Danish Defence of its decision to make a warship, a cargo ship and management and personnel available to the operation. At the same time, the Norwegian Navy had volunteered a warship and, as needed, a cargo ship should it prove necessary to have two ships to convey the many tons of chemical substances.

Admiral Danish Fleet (SOK), Rear Admiral Frank Trojahn, would have supreme operational command of the operation. Tactical command of the operation would not be based at the SOK headquarters in Aarhus but would rest with a force commander and staff appointed to head the operation from one of the Navy's ships in the mission area. A task of this kind is usually assigned to the Commander of Danish Task Group, a

The Danish Task Group (STS), the Danish Navy's tactical staff element, was established in 2000. Here they are depicted during an exercise in 2016. Until 2019, the STS was responsible for heading up international naval forces in missions such as the anti-piracy operations off the Horn of Africa. In connection with an organisational restructuring of the Navy in 2019, the STS was incorporated into the Navy Command in Karup, and today personnel for international operations are drawn from all relevant parts of the Navy.

The leadership of the Danish Navy briefly considered using one of the Navy's inspection vessels of the Thetis class as command ship in the operation, but it soon became clear that threat assessments of the situation in the waters off Syria required a warship better equipped for self-defence and battle. Esbern Snare, *one of the Navy's two support ships, was therefore chosen for the task. With a displacement of 6,300 tons, it is one of the largest units ever commanded by the Danish Navy. Together with the Navy's frigates of the Iver Huitfeldt class, these ships have been built specifically for operations far from Danish waters and have on several occasions been deployed to the anti-piracy operations off the Horn of Africa.* Esbern Snare *is armed with a 127-millimetre cannon, anti-ship and anti-aircraft missiles and a series of short-range defence systems, just as it can house up to two helicopters. It ordinarily accommodates a crew of approx. 113, but its berth accommodation allows for as many as 165.*

permantly established Task Group Commander and Staff established in 2000 do perform exaetly such task, i.e. leading maritime Task Groups. However, the Danish Task Group Commander, commondore Aage Buur Jensen, and some of his staff were at the time deployed to lead one of the naval forces involved in the international anti-piracy mission off the Horn of Africa. Instead, I was appointed force commander, supported by the remaining members of the Navy's Tactical Staff, other authorities in the Danish Navy and a number of foreign partners. At the time, I was Chief of the Navy's Second Squadron based in Korsør. My staff would include officers from the US, Sweden, Norway and Great Britain, with Norwegian Commander Svein Erik Kvalvaag serving as Chief of Staff.

The Royal Danish Naval Academy teaches us that we as officers must fill three roles: the warrior, the leader and the diplomat. Even though the three roles overlap, it is the role of the warrior that has attracted most attention in the course of the Danish Navy's 500-year history while the other two elements have, more or less, been allowed to slip into the background. Already at an early stage, I realised that in this operation I would – hopefully – come to make more use of my skills as a diplomat and leader rather than as a warrior. At the strategic level, actors from both Denmark, Norway, Russia, China, Syria, Great Britain, Finland, Sweden, the US and, not least, the UN and OPCW would participate in the mission.

At the tactical level, one of the most exciting aspects was the fact that the Danish contribution to the operation consisted of elements from various Danish organisations and agencies. Thus, in addition to Navy personnel, the operation would also draw on specialists in chemical, biological, radioactive and nuclear (CBRN) material from the Danish Emergency Management Agency and the Danish Army, as well as staff officers from both the Army and the Danish Air Force and personnel from the Danish Customs and Tax Administration. The latter was responsible for operating the mobile container scanner brought along to X-ray the containers holding chemical agents before they were loaded onto the cargo ships.

When we first started to plan the operation, our first challenge was the Navy's limited knowledge of Syria. Such knowledge had not been necessary in previous work, so we very much began with a blank slate. My staff simply began by searching the Internet for information on very basic things like: What is Syria's Mediterranean geography like? Which ports could act as potential ports of disembarkation? How deep are these ports? And so on. Once we had acquired this knowledge, we could look for information about the ongoing conflict: Who controlled the various areas? Where were they fighting at present? How many warships, missiles, airplanes, field guns etc. did the different parties in the civil war have at their disposal? All basic information that was necessary in order to gain an overview of the situation.

It soon became clear to us that the chemical agents would probably have to be collected from the Syrian port of Latakia, and we then went on to simple tasks like obtaining charts of the waters off Latakia and a map of the port itself.

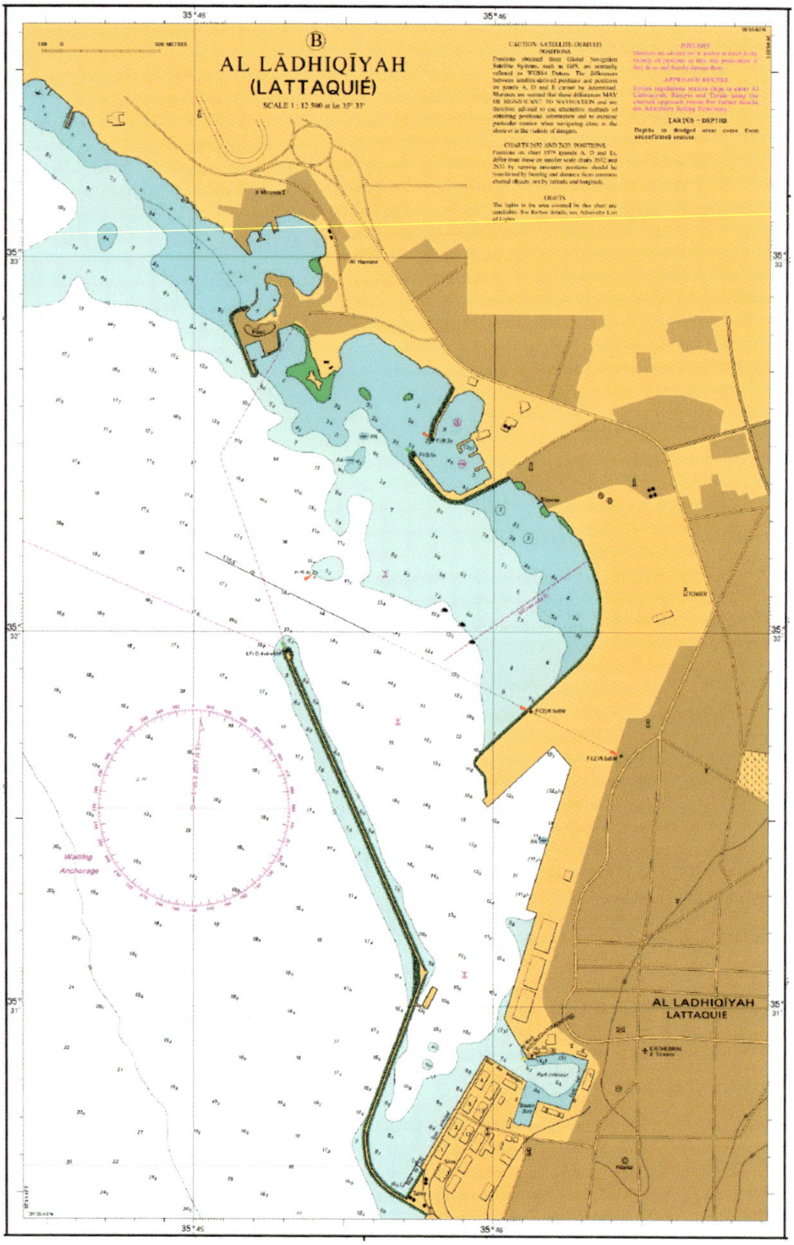

Latakia is the fourth largest city in Syria and the country's largest port. It is located approx. 350 kilometres from the capital of Damascus. Throughout the civil war, it had been controlled by the Syrian regime and only seen very little fighting. However, in the autumn of 2013 fighting took place not far from the city, fighting which we would come to experience at close range during Operation RECSYR. (Crown Copyright 2019)

Having solved these tasks, we could now begin to ask more direct questions about the conditions in the area – the so-called Commander's Critical Information Requirements (CCIR), which comprised the commander's, that is, my list of information necessary to execute the operation. This included a threat assessment for Latakia, the Syrian population's view of the mission, al-Assad's control over the forces around Latakia, the extent of Russia's presence and the like.

Subsequently, the staff began to plan the actual mission and to answer practical questions such as: What should we bring along? How would we reach the mission area? Whom would we bring? And so forth.

In other words, we had to do a lot of coordination involving a large number of people on various levels, inside as well as outside of the Danish Defence. Our eventual success was due not least to the favour and tremendous support we received from everyone involved.

A delicate matter was the fact that collecting the chemical substances in Latakia required operating in Syrian territorial waters and on Syrian territory. We therefore had to cooperate with the Syrian forces loyal to the Government, which according to the UN Resolution were to safeguard the personnel of the participating nations when present within Syrian territory.

I thus had to cooperate with the Syrian forces loyal to the Government in a way that both showed them the necessary respect and ensured that I would not be grovelling to al-Assad's forces nor compromising either the safety of my forces or our ability to complete the mission. This delicate balancing act was further challenged by the fact that we did not have a complete picture of what to expect of the overall situation in and off Latakia. Here, I had to choose between the warrior and the diplomat as my main role. If I let the warrior decide, the most appropriate strategy would be to arrive in Latakia and to operate inside the port with a very robust and visible military force. However, the Syrians might consider this to indicate that I did not trust them to be in charge of the security situation in the port. A robust approach might therefore provoke them and thus undermine our cooperation with the Syrian forces in the city, thereby endangering the entire mission.

I chose a balanced and diplomatic approach and asked my staff to devise a plan that would not have been much different had we instead been tasked with entering peaceful Copenhagen to collect a couple of containers with chemical agents. For example, this decision meant that when we arrived in Latakia we would let the cargo ships enter the port first, followed by a Danish or Norwegian warship. If I had let the warrior decide, the warship would have entered the port first, protecting the cargo ships from potential threats. But this way I showed Syria the necessary respect and that I trusted their security guarantees. Yet at the same time, I always had the necessary combat power at my disposal to respond to sudden threats, e.g. by letting special forces from the Danish Frogman Corps or the Norwegian Coastal Ranger Command enter the port first in fast vessels to reconnoitre the area for potential threats before the cargo ships and warships entered the port. This also enabled us to inspect the pilot vessel and tugboats: Were they in fact pilot vessels and tugboats or something else entirely? We were also able to inspect the piers and the approach before calling at port. The overall need for maximum security for ships and crew and the consideration for the Syrian authorities in Latakia represented a constant balancing act.

As a minor detail, we referred to the warships as Consequence Management Response Units (CMRU) and not Military Escorts, precisely because the term CMRU points to the ships' defensive role, which is not necessarily the case with the term Military Escort. This would later turn out to be a wise decision.

It was decided that the Danish contribution would consist of the support ship *Esbern Snare* and the civilian cargo ship *Ark Futura*. Seeing as it had served as Denmark's contribution to the anti-piracy operation off the Horn of Africa since September 2013, *Esbern Snare* was already present in the area. It would not take long for the ship to reach the eastern Mediterranean, and on 6 December the support ship made for Cyprus where it would meet up with the rest of the participating units. *Esbern Snare* was thus already on its way to the eastern Mediterranean when the Danish Parliament made the formal decision to make the ship available to Operation RECSYR. Had this not been the case, the ship would not have been able to reach the mission area on time; and had a majority in the Parliament chosen not to deploy the ship, it would simply have turned around and returned to the area off the Horn of Africa. This is a good example of the flexibility inherent to naval units. They can be deployed to international waters without diplomatic consequences and thereby prepare for a mission or turn around and head back, depending on the political process and the result of other possible solutions.

On 12 October 2000, the American destroyer Cole *was attacked while refuelling in the Yemenite port of Aden. An innocent-looking motorboat pulled alongside of the ship, and suicide terrorists on board the boat subsequently detonated a bomb of somewhere between 180 and 320 kilos. The bomb blew a 12-by-18-metre hole in the hull of the ship, killed 17 of the ship's 281-member crew and wounded 39. Despite the extensive damage, the ship was repaired, and after two years in the shipyard the* Cole *re-entered service in the US Navy. Threats like these very much had our attention during Operation RECSYR. This photo of the* Cole *on its way to the shipyard in the US on board the cargo ship MV* Blue Marlin *clearly shows the hole on the port side of the destroyer. (P.S. Draham/Ritzau/Scanpix)*

Ark Futura is a civilian cargo ship that since 2003 has formed part of the Danish Navy's so-called ARK project. The aim of the project is to provide the Danish Navy and NATO with a much-needed capacity for strategic maritime transport – that is, the ability with short notice to help the Alliance move e.g. a larger ground force from Europe to a mission area. The idea emerged after the NATO summit in Prague in 2012, where the Alliance established the NATO Response Force – a large, multinational force capable of being deployed with short notice to more or less any part of the world. In order to deploy this force, however, the NATO member states had to have transport capacity at their disposal. The Danish Government therefore chose to enter into an agreement with the Danish shipping company DFDS to lease its cargo ships. According to the agreement, the ships form part of the company's normal transportation network, but the Danish Defence and NATO have a right to use the ships when required. They only have to pay for the ships when they actually use them, securing the ARK project the best possible financial solution.

When the need for more ships arose, the number of ships was increased until the Danish Defence in 2014 – together with the Germany Navy – commanded five roll-on/roll-off ships.

As part of our preparation for RECSYR, DFDS was informed on 9 December that the Navy wished to use *Ark Futura* for an operation in the Mediterranean. Initially, we expected the pickups to last from 15 December 2013 to the end of the year, and thus to be able to return *Ark Futura* to DFDS at the end of January 2014. The mission would turn out to take much longer than this, however.

Concurrently with our preparations, the Norwegian Navy was also preparing for the mission. The frigate *Helge Ingstad* was designated as the Norwegian military contribution to the operation. To ensure the necessary flexibility, we wanted to have two cargo ships at our disposal – for two reasons. First, we wanted to prevent situations where e.g. a serious breakdown of *Ark Futura* would cause delays in the pickup of chemical agents in the port of Latakia. Second, it made good sense not to compile all the chemical agents in one location. Before use, the chemical agents had to be mixed with actual warfare gasses, and if we were able to place e.g. the components for the sarin gas on separate ships, this would minimise the risk that they might, as a result of spillage, mix and turn into very dangerous gasses.

As the Norwegian Navy did not have an ARK project similar to the Danish programme, the Ministry of Foreign Affairs of Norway had to charter a civilian cargo ship for the job. They chose the cargo ship *Taiko* belonging to the Norwegian shipping company Wilhelmsen Lines. *Taiko* is considerably larger than *Ark Futura*, but a ship of the same type, namely a so-called roll-on/roll-off ship with a large aft loading ramp, which facilitates easy loading and unloading of containers carried by trailers.

In connection with Operation RECSYR, *Taiko* was reflagged, giving it the status of a Norwegian state-owned ship. According to international law, a state-owned ship cannot be detained, and representatives of other states are not allowed to board such a ship without the captain's

The Norwegian Navy made the frigate Helge Ingstad *available to Operation RECSYR. On board the frigate of the Fridtjof Nansen class was a crew of approx. 180, while the Danish ship,* Esbern Snare, *had a crew of approx. 130.* Helge Ingstad *was a state-of-the-art and potent warship. Regrettably, it sank on 8 November 2018 – fortunately with no casualties – after colliding with a Maltese tanker near Bergen. (L.M. Hovtun/ Forsvaret.no)*

permission. This also applies when the ship is in foreign territorial waters. State-owned ship status thus gave *Taiko* a number of advantages in connection with our operations in Syrian waters, just as the crew on board *Taiko* enjoyed greater legal protection than the crew on other civilian ships. Defence Command Denmark chose not to reflag *Ark Futura*, however, and it therefore remained a civilian cargo ship with everything this entails, e.g. allowing the Syrians access to inspect the ship. I wanted to provide the ship and its crew with the best possible protection, and I thus had to invest considerable time and resources making the Syrians accept that *Ark Futura* de facto would enjoy the same status as *Taiko*. I was successful, but it would have saved us a lot of trouble if Defence Command Denmark had chosen to reflag *Ark Futura*. On the other hand, the fact that *Ark Futura* had not been reflagged turned out to be an advantage in other contexts, as it made it less difficult for the ship to approach foreign ports to load the chemical substances and carry them to destruction facilities.

Exercise in evacuation of contaminated personnel from Ark Futura.

Concurrently with our preparations, Syrian forces – supervised by the OPCW – loaded the chemical agents into containers. This work took place in 13 locations throughout Syria, and the containers then had to be transported to Latakia, where we would pick them up. The OPCW staff did not travel with the containers through the civil war-ridden country. That would have been too dangerous. Instead, the containers were sealed and equipped with GPS trackers, enabling the OPCW staff to monitor their progress through the country. Upon arriving in Latakia, the OPCW staff examined the containers to see if the seal had been broken and carried out spot checks to determine whether the content had been tampered with.

To me as commander of the naval force, the fact that the chemical agents would, after having been packed and sealed, travel through Syria without supervision by the OPCW, for example, constituted a challenge. Several of the Syrian rebel forces had expressed an intent to attack the lorries, as they would consider it a victory for President al-Assad if the chemical agents managed to escape Syria. We feared that the people who wanted to sabotage the operation or hurt us might open the containers and place explosives inside before resealing them, making it impossible for us to see that they had been opened. As a rule, we were only allowed to open the containers in case of an emergency. We solved this challenge by borrowing a mobile container scanner from the Danish Customs and Tax Administration. This scanner is a lorry fitted with a huge X-ray machine that can unfold as a gantry, allowing the container to pass through the portal. The machine can 'see' through armoured steel, and if we saw anything suspicious in the images, we could take a closer look and, where relevant, refuse to load the container onto the ship. In addition, we had at our disposal an explosives detection dog whose sharp nose was trained to sniff out explosives.

Several of the roads to Latakia were seeing violent fighting at the time, so the containers might very well have bullet holes and similar damage when they arrived in Latakia. We also had with us several chemical specialists who would, among other things, check each container for spills.

Aside from the political and military challenges, the fact that Syria in the winter of 2013/2014 saw the worst snowfall in years further complicated the mission, as the Syrians were completely unprepared for this type of weather. They neither had snowploughs nor equipment for salting, which further delayed the transport.

A tanker carrying chemical agents passing through one of the Danish Customs and Tax Administration's mobile container scanners. The photo was taken in August 2016 in the Libyan port of Misrata during Operation RECLIB – an operation which in many ways resembled Operation RECSYR. Ark Futura *is seen in the background. (T. Hein)*

On December 10, I boarded *Esbern Snare* in the port of Limassol in Cyprus along with the rest of the staff. Some of the staff members had been involved in planning the operation, along with a British and a US chief of staff, at the Korsør Naval Base. The following is an excerpt from my journal detailing our preparation in the period 10-24 December 2013:

> Since 10 December, when the staff boarded *Esbern Snare*, we have been very busy preparing for the job of collecting chemical agents from Syria. The ships in the force have trained both individually and together and made a great effort to develop procedures for this specific task. We have been joined by Finnish specialists in chemical, biological, radiological and nuclear weapons and the equivalent from the Danish Army and Emergency Management Agency, including a research chemist and four employees from the Danish Customs and Tax Administration, who will operate the mobile scanner on board the Danish cargo ship, *Ark Futura*, which will transport the chemical agents together with its Norwegian colleague, the cargo ship *Taiko*. Task Group 420.01, which is the official name of the naval force that I command, thus consists of the Norwegian frigate *Helge Ingstad*, the Danish flagship *Esbern Snare*, the Danish cargo ship *Ark Futura* and the Norwegian cargo ship *Taiko*. In total, the naval force comprises around 350 personnel. These include specialists in chemical agents, Norwegian coastal rangers on *Taiko*, providing it with armed protection, and members of the Danish Frogman Corps tasked with protecting *Ark Futura* and its crew. My staff consists of hard-working Danish, Norwegian and Finnish officers. During the planning phase, British and American officers were also involved in the mission. However, as they are not allowed into Syrian territorial waters, they cannot form part of the staff once we set out to collect the chemical substances. In the period 10-19 December 2013, we conducted what we call Force Integration Training, developing internal procedures as well as procedures for helping each other in case of an emergency. Here we mainly focus on supporting the cargo ships in emergencies, e.g. fire, accidents on board, a container leaking chemical agents and, the worst-case scenarios: a terrorist attack against the ships in the port or at sea, or explosives having been planted in one of the containers that we have taken on board.

The day I boarded *Esbern Snare*, the Danish Parliament completed its first reading of the political foundation for our participation in the operation, and motion 'B 29 on the Danish Contribution to the UN and OPCW Mission in Syria' (see the Appendix) was passed on the 19th of that month.

The latter made a flexible support ship, up to two cargo ships, a naval command team of up to 20 individuals, an unspecified number of naval special forces from the Danish Frogman Corps, one of the Danish Air Force's C-130 transport aircraft and a personal protection team of 19 to protect Dutch UN diplomat Sigrid Kaag available to the operation. It was estimated that the Danish contribution would cost around DKK 60 million, which was to be absorbed by the Danish Defence.

The Danish contribution to the UN-OPCW mission in Syria

The naval contribution was to consist of:

- Up to two cargo ships
- A flexible support ship of the Absalon class
- Plus a naval command team

A total of up to 250 individuals. Added to this was a small number of naval special forces

The air transport contribution was to consist of:

- A C-130J transport aircraft

A total of up to 25 individuals.

The motion was passed with 97 votes in favour and 14 against. The naysayers came from the Danish People's Party, who supported the deployment of Danish ships, but not the deployment of a Danish personal protection team. These lightly armed Danish soldiers would operate on Syrian soil in cooperation with al-Assad's forces, and the Danish People's Party did not wish to lend their support to such cooperation, and they therefore chose to vote against the motion.

The Moscow Plan

The original OPCW plan was to collect the first containers in Latakia on 15 December 2013. We therefore hurried to get ready, but on 14 December we had to realise that the Syrians had been delayed and would not be ready until 19 December at the earliest.

This did not come as a surprise. Right from the outset, we had operated with 27 December as the most likely starting date for the operation. However, the mission was further delayed by high politics, as China and Russia had realised that active participation in removing the chemical weapons from Syria would provide them with a series of obvious advantages. Russia in particular was very interested in keeping al-Assad on as president of Syria. The Russians made their support of the operation clear by having the Russian Navy send its flagship, the cruiser *Pyotr Velikiy*, from Severomorsk at Murmansk to the eastern Mediterranean.

The Chinese Government did not have any direct interests in Syria. Nevertheless, it did wish to support international order and considered participation in Operation RECSYR as a way to assert itself as a global superpower. The Chinese Government thus announced that it would send the frigate *Yancheng* to the waters off Syria.

Even though the Russian and Chinese ships would not form a direct part of my force, it was clear to everyone that we had to find a way to cooperate. The Ministry of Foreign Affairs of the Russian Federation thus invited us to a tactical planning meeting in Moscow on 27 December. At the meeting, I would brief the Russians, Chinese and Syrians of our plan for collecting the chemical agents. The official reason for the meeting was the three parties' wish to contribute to protecting the cargo ships in Syrian territorial waters, but in my opinion their main interest was to keep an eye on us and to learn how we intended to operate. This did not make a difference, however, because as long as we were allowed to protect and support our ships and crews in the way we saw fit, the Syrians could have as many ships in the area as they wanted to. Our only absolute demand was that *Esbern Snare* and/or *Helge Ingstad* were allowed to enter Syrian territorial waters to support *Ark Futura* and *Taiko* if necessary. Via the UN envoy, Astrid Kaag, I pushed for the Syrian

Pyotr Velikiy *(Peter the Great) of the Kirov class was built during the Cold War and is currently the largest and most potent warship sailing the oceans. It is nuclear-powered, has a crew of more than 700 and a displacement of 28,000 tons, which is more than twice the total displacement tonnage of* Esbern Snare *and* Helge Ingstad *put together. In the air above the cruiser is* Esbern Snare's *Lynx helicopter.*

Government's official permission to operate in Syrian territorial waters, and Astrid – whom I spoke to so many times that we are now on first-name terms – promised me that this would be in order before the meeting in Moscow. She kept her word, and the day before the meeting, I received a letter from the Syrian Deputy Foreign Minister, giving us permission to enter Syrian territorial waters with Danish and Norwegian warships to carry out this specific task. Much can be achieved when you have the right people working on it.

While I prepared for the trip to Moscow, I decided that the units in my force (together referred to as Task Group 420.01) would call at Limassol in Cyprus. The first training had been successfully completed, and we could now spend the next three days refuelling, relaxing and taking on

On 15 December we received a visit from the Danish Minister of Defence, Nicolai Wammen, the Cypriot Minister of Defence, the Danish Ambassador in Cyprus, Casper Klynge, and Chief of the Naval Command, Rear Admiral Frank Trojahn. I gather you could call this a VIP-day at sea.

board provisions so that we could be ready if the need suddenly arose. I decided that the units should operate at a 12-hour emergency readiness, as I expected us to be given a 24-hour warning before a pickup. This 12-hour emergency readiness meant that we could be in place in the port of Latakia no later than 12 hours after we had been given a green light to launch Operation RECSYR – as I believed it would take us one hour to leave Limassol, 10 hours to cover the approx. 170 nautical miles between Limassol and Latakia and one hour for the cargo ships to call at the port. This meant that the atmosphere on the ships was cheerful, as the crews could relax and even go ashore for a bit to escape the cramped spaces on board.

After three days in Limassol, we put out to sea again, where we continued our Force Enhancement Training. The crews had to be ready in case of an attack on one of the ships, but also to handle a chemical spill, which was not something we were used to training. I am convinced that everyone could see the purpose of the mission and was highly motivated both for the training and the mission itself.

In order to minimise wear on the crew and spouses and children back home, the crew on *Esbern Snare* would rotate home following three months' deployment. As the ship had come directly from the anti-piracy operation off the Horn of Africa, where it had been since September 2013, we had slightly postponed the turnover to mid-January 2014. The crew of more than 120 individuals had on short notice managed to shift their focus from fighting piracy to chemical emergency readiness. They were very talented, and I very much hoped to be able to collect at least one shipment of chemical agents before the crew rotation so that the many hours of training and the professional shift in focus would not feel like a complete waste of time.

Before I was able to leave for Moscow, there was one important thing we had to do: celebrate Christmas Eve.

24 December 2013

Today, my Norwegian Deputy Commander and I visited the units to wish them a Merry Christmas. They had been told that Santa and his helper would be dropping by if they had been nice. This was course the case, so I dressed up as Santa, and with a sack of gifts slung over one shoulder, I jumped into the Frogman Corps' dinghy, which I then used as a 'sleigh'. I visited all the units, shook everyone's hand and wished them Merry Christmas. I was hard at work climbing up and down the large cargo ships, eight stories up and eight stories down the ladders, and hanging on at a speed of approx. 50 knots in decent waves. But it was great fun.

'Swim call' is the naval expression for bathing in the sea.

When we returned to *Esbern Snare*, we still had an hour before we had to dance around the Christmas tree on the helicopter deck. We were anchored in formation, and the crew of the Norwegian frigate was on swim call (the water temperature was 19 degrees Celsius). The Minister of Defence handed out Christmas presents, and from 17:00-19:00 we ate Christmas dinner, before relaxing with Christmas candy and a film in the mess. A good day, which all things considered, did resemble a traditional Danish Christmas Eve.

Personally, I spent the last hours of the day adjusting the overall plan of the operation and drawing up directives for the next 24 hours for the four ships, before giving my superior, Rear Admiral Frank Trojahn, in the Naval Command in Aarhus an update of the situation.

At the same time, I was expecting a call from home. I missed my family and was eager to learn whether my gifts had been well received. They had, and around midnight I went to sleep.

I had called the commanders of the other ships to a meeting at 07:30 on 25 December, where we would go over the content of my Moscow presentation. I wanted their input to make sure that I would be presenting a consolidated Danish/Norwegian proposal. The last thing I wanted was to present something that had not been 'cleared' internally.

Santa on the helicopter deck of Esbern Snare, *with Limassol in the background.*

25 December 2013

I woke at 06:45 and was ready for the meeting at 07:30. The others managed to board the ship without problems, even though the waves had increased overnight. The waves were 1.5 metres high, which can make it difficult to get from a dinghy and onto the ladders.

It has been a quiet day, and we have given the commanders time to relax and do whatever they feel like.

The staff has had the usual meetings. The morning meeting, the midday synchronisation meeting, and tonight I will do my daily briefing of the staff – the so-called Command Team Briefing. We usually speak English for the sake of our foreign staff members.

Today the helicopter has been out supporting the Norwegian frigate, which has not brought a helicopter of its own. It has been practising landing and refuelling etc. In return, they refuelled the helicopter before returning it to *Esbern Snare*. ☺

Today I have spent time optimising and perfecting the briefing I will be giving in Russia. We will only be given this one shot, so it has to be perfect. Once I am done, we will translate it into a Russian PowerPoint. I think this will pay off at the meeting.

Today has been a quiet day on the ship. The crew need a rest. They have just spent three months at sea, whereas the rest of us have newly arrived with motivation and zest. Tonight we played bingo. Regrettably, I did not win anything.

Later I wrote the usual directives and progress reports. Finally, I prepared the written material for the Moscow meeting and packed to make sure I will be ready to leave in the morning.

26 December 2013

Today we will leave for Moscow. I am anxious about how they will receive my presentation. This is a high-politics game which I am involved in here, and there is a long way to fall if you make a fool of yourself! I do not think that will happen, though. I will stick to the tactical aspects and the requirements I recognise with regard to solving the task, and leave the politics to someone else. Nevertheless, I did not expect to have to go to Moscow for such a meeting in order to complete the task. But apparently this is what it takes, and so be it. I would have preferred to have stayed on board, but seeing as the meeting concerns the tactical aspects and the way we will be solving the task, there is probably no way of avoiding it.

Around noon, the Frogman Corps took me into Limassol, where I continued to the airport and flew to Moscow together with Carsten (a military lawyer), David (a military linguist specialising in Russian) and Søren (a planning officer from the staff). After some scowling by the passport control in Moscow, I was allowed to enter on my diplomatic passport. The Russians do not like to allow foreigners without a visa into the country, which is usually the case for diplomats. And they were not informed of the purpose of my visit, so they were a bit suspicious. It did go okay, though, despite the hassle. A driver was waiting for us at the airport, and he took us to the Hotel Lotte at the centre of Moscow. Wow, what a hotel. I have never seen such large rooms and so much Christmas bling. Very impressive, I must say. We arrived at 20:00 and went to the restaurant for a bite to eat before turning in.

The Meeting in Moscow

The day started with a brief breakfast meeting with Denmark's Chief of Naval Staff, Frank Trojahn, and Commander Pet Moll, who acted as our liaison officer to the OPCW mission headquarters in Cyprus. They had both arrived the previous day. Also present was the Danish defence attaché in Moscow, Brigadier Lennie Fredskov.

I had not slept well that night, as I had started to realise the scale of the affair of which I had become part.

While we were coordinating the day's work over breakfast, an American major general from the US European Command in Stuttgart arrived. As previously mentioned, the US did not have anything to do with the part of the operation that would take place in Syrian territorial waters, but would participate in the destruction process on *Cape Ray*. They were therefore interested in this part of the mission. The major general was also there to show US support for the mission. After talking briefly to the American major general, we continued coordinating the day's events, and the plan was that Frank Trojahn would give a short introduction outlining the main messages. Subsequently, I would present our plan.

When we arrived at the meeting venue – an impressive location in the centre of Moscow – few had shown up. The meeting room had been equipped with a huge table with around 45 name signs, including that of the Russian Deputy Foreign Minister, Sergey Ryabkov. Then the three large delegations from Russia, China and Syria, respectively, arrived, as did a US general. I realised that we would be speaking English, Russian, Arabic and Chinese, and that constant simultaneous interpretation would be available via headphones. The Russian Deputy Foreign Minister opened the meeting and then yielding the floor to a Russian colonel, who presented the Russian/Chinese plan. The main idea was that the Russians and Syrians would be responsible for protecting the cargo ships in Syrian territorial waters, and we would only be escorting *Ark Futura* and *Taiko* to the territorial border, where Syrian naval ships – supported by Russian ships – would take over the escort of the cargo ships and make sure they arrived in the port safely. This plan was very different from ours, as we wanted to escort our cargo ships safely into the port ourselves.

After the Russian presentation, it was our turn, and as agreed Frank Trojahn began before giving me the floor. I went through my 20 very detailed PowerPoint slides, outlining the stages of the operation. After my presentation, the Deputy Foreign Minister concluded that we now had to synchronise the two plans to arrive at a joint plan. We, the Danish team, conferred briefly and drew up a coordinated plan on a piece of paper.

It became clear that both the Russians, Chinese and Syrians felt that there was a serious possibility that the cargo ships would be attacked by smaller boats upon entering or leaving the port of Latakia. The Russians therefore wanted to place warships both north and south of the port in order to detect a possible attack before it became a threat to the cargo ships. The waters off Latakia would therefore be divided into a northern and southern sector, and my force would cover the northern one while the Russians and the Chinese would cover the southern sector, with Syrian missile torpedo boats patrolling the Syrian coastline close to shore. We could agree to this part of their plan, but I maintained that the Danish and Norwegian warships would continue to escort the two cargo ships after they entered Syrian waters and the port.

With our plan in my hand, I got ready at one end of the room to discuss and synchronise the two plans. But I was completely ignored, as the

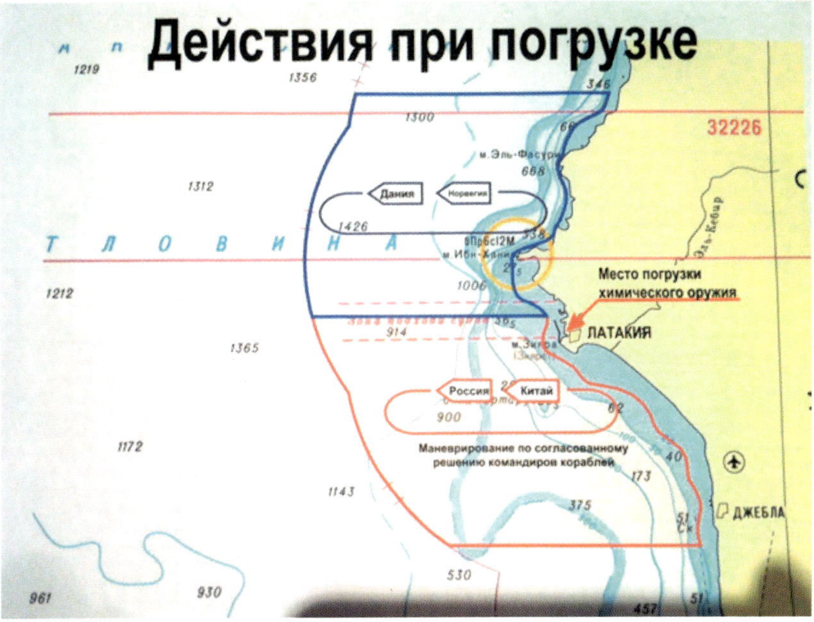

Russian PowerPoint of the Russian plan for the collection of chemical agents in Latakia. It shows the Danish/Norwegian sector at the top and the Russian/Chinese sector at the bottom.

Chinese, Russians and Syrians went to a different table at the other end of the room to discuss their own proposal.

After some time, they came up to me to synchronise the plans, and suddenly I was surrounded by a crowd of around 45 people. The Russians and Chinese then presented their proposal once again, not differing from the one they had already presented. I then showed them our proposal which to a certain extent united the plans without compromising with our wish to protect the two cargo ships at all times.

Seeing as I only had two warships in my force, and seeing as chemical agents would eventually be loaded onto both cargo ships, I would be unable to leave them, which would make them vulnerable targets. Each cargo ship should constantly be under the protection of at least one warship. If I had to cover the northern sector, my only option was to move the holding area where we would be waiting for shipments of chemical agents closer to the coast, as this would enable us to cover the northern sector in connection with pickups in Latakia. This would increase the risk of a potential land-based missile threat, reduce the time of warning

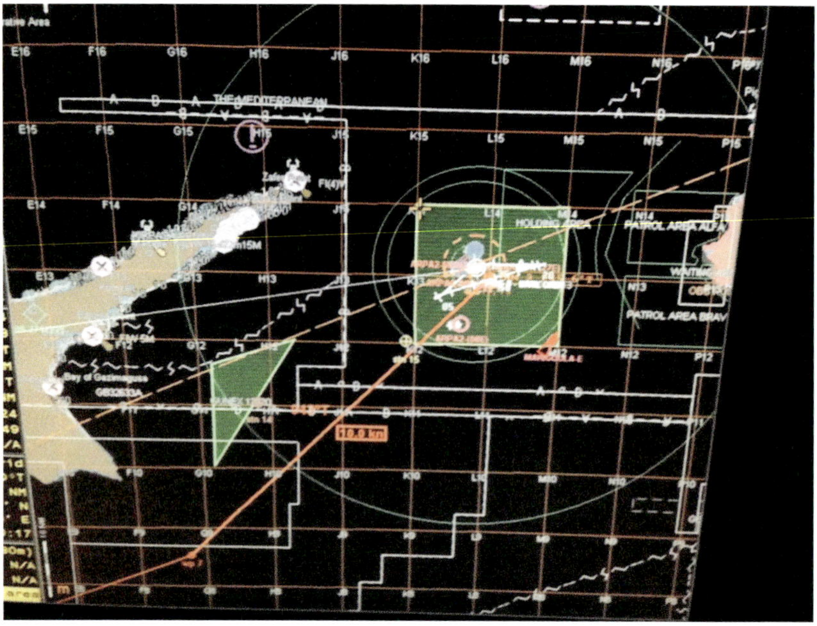

The holding area shown by the green square was approximately halfway between the easternmost tip of Cyprus and the Syrian coast. (R.R. Nicolaisen)

in case of an attack and increase the distance to our logistical base in Limassol in Cyprus. All in all, though, this was not something we could not handle.

Finally, I concluded by saying that my force was able to cover the northern sector from the holding area, and that we had permission to enter Syrian territorial waters if necessary. I was thus able to counter a potential threat to the ships.

I used the opportunity to mention that my force would be joined by a British warship, and that this unit would support the mission, though without entering Syrian territorial waters. It was important to mention this aspect at this point to ensure that it would not cause trouble later on.

The Syrians then informed us that they would make one or two minor warships available for patrolling the northern sector, making the total protection capacity more robust than the one we alone could have provided. This meant that I neither had to compromise on our need for operating in Syrian territorial waters nor on our need for operating inside and outside the port with small boats, and that the final plan was a rather good one.

The participating British warship was the frigate Montrose, *here seen together with* Ark Futura *and* Helge Ingstad *in the background. (MoD)*

Several times during the negotiations I had to supress the 'warrior' in me and focus on the 'diplomat'. I did so successfully, and the result was a positive one. I am convinced that our detailed plan and knowledge of the many aspects of the operation were the reasons why the final plan was based on our initial one. The plan was merely improved, as actual operational support from Russian, Chinese and Syrian units was added to it. To be honest, the meeting gave me a bit of a buzz, and I was proud of the positive outcome.

Subsequently, the Syrians asked a series of questions, mainly about how I intended to act in various situations. If we were attacked with artillery or mortars from positions in Syria, would we defend ourselves by shooting at the attackers on shore? My answer was: No, not at first. Initially, we would act in self-defence by leaving the port as fast as possible, but of course self-defence also includes the use of lethal force. And if compelled, I would resort to said use of force by attacking positions in Syria. This did not cause them to flinch. They informed me that they would have divers patrolling the port and that explosives would be detonated regularly below the surface to keep potential enemy divers away. We were therefore asked not to use our own divers.

I then suggested that we update our PowerPoint slides, adjusting them to reflect the joint plan. And while I ate lunch, my staff officers set to work adjusting our original briefing. An hour later, we had a more or less final plan, which we then presented.

Nevertheless, the meeting almost ended in disaster when we announced that we naturally could not rule out situations where we would be forced to deviate from the plan. We were ready for the operation, and if we suddenly received the green light, it would not be expedient to have to wait for the Russian and Chinese warships to arrive in the waters off Latakia. This immediately created a negative atmosphere in the room, as neither Russia nor China is used to great flexibility in military operations. Once they have drawn up a plan, it must be followed, without changes and with central control from Moscow or Beijing.

The chairmen of the meeting said something about 'reliable partners' working together and 'on this negative note' etc. We then argued that the changes required might be *minor* ones, and we thus managed to get all the participating nations to sign the plan dubbed the Moscow Plan.

On our way back, my experience of the meeting caused me to write a letter to the commanders of the Russian, Chinese and Syrian ships that would participate in the operation. The letter, which was sent to the embassies of the respective countries, read as follows:

Dear reliable partners, dear friends,
Please allow me to express my gratitude for our common work and especially our common achievements during our meeting in Moscow on December 27, 2013.

I am impressed by the fact that our nations – by us working together – succeeded in synchronizing the Russian/Chinese/Syrian plan and the Danish/Norwegian/Finnish plan into one multinational plan – quickly and smoothly – based on our common understanding of what needed to be achieved.

This was only possible because we are all professionals and want to work together for this good cause.

As you know, the Danish/Norwegian Task Group is reported full mission capable and ready to execute on short notice. We will be operating in the eastern part of the Mediterranean and will also deploy to the agreed holding area outside Syrian territorial waters, where we will conduct Force Enhancement Training until called upon.

I found it very inspiring to meet you all in Moscow and I am sure our future cooperation will be an inspiration to us all.

Until we meet again, I would like to wish you seven feet under your keel.

With regards,
Torben Mikkelsen
Commodore
Commander Task Group 420.01

The purpose of the letter was to demonstrate openness and to ensure that the cooperation at my level between myself, the commanders of the other ships and the Syrian forces ashore would be as frictionless as possible. After all, the task had to be solved at the tactical level, and I did not want any friction here. Problems would emerge, yes, but the more we were able to nip in the bud, the better.

Waiting Time

I returned to *Esbern Snare* on the evening of 28 December. The ship had been waiting for us in the port of Limassol, and shortly after we had arrived it put out to sea to join the other ships in the force, which had been waiting at sea. As *Esbern Snare* left the port, I received a series of calls from the Naval Command in Aarhus, but each time I tried to return their call I found that the number was engaged. When I finally managed to get through, I spoke to the operation commander on watch, who had been the one making the calls. He had heard on the news that we were on our way to Latakia to collect the first shipment of chemical agents. He just wanted to know if this was correct. This made me pretty cross, and I informed him that, first of all, they knew exactly what we were doing at any given time. We constantly sent home signals and reports. Second, but just as important, I informed him that I expected the Naval Command to trust me in my capacity as commander, and that of course I would not leave for Syria without informing them. Third, I told him that the preconditions for entering Syria to collect a shipment of chemical agents were not there yet. Among other things, a loading port had not been identified yet. Fourth, neither Russia nor China was ready yet – after all, we had just met with them in Moscow to discuss the plan.

The main room on board a contemporary warship is the combat information centre (CIC). Here information from all the sensors on board and from friendly units is compiled, and this is where the commander of the ship leads the battle, if it should come to that. (T. Wismann)

In hindsight, I was probably unnecessarily harsh with the commander on watch. After all, he just wanted to make sure that he had the right information, and he probably became the object of my frustration because I felt his question suggested that the Naval Command did not trust me to execute the task competently. The Naval Command had made me commander and thus given me the authority to complete the operation as I saw best. I felt that the many questions they asked, time and again, undermined my authority and that if they did not trust me, they were free to give the job to someone else.

Granted, the operation commander on watch was just a messenger, and I regret taking my frustration out on him. At this point in time, Frank Trojahn had yet to return from Moscow, and back home in Aarhus they probably just wanted to make sure that everything went well during his absence.

We spent the night training communications between the information centres on *Esbern Snare* and *Helge Ingstad*, respectively, and on sailing in formation, training protection of *Ark Futura* and *Taiko*. The training continued the following days, where we trained both attacks on the force and handling accidents involving chemical agents on board *Ark Futura* or *Taiko*.

***Esbern Snare's* 'Battle Rhythm' During Operation RECSYR**

When on mission, the crew of a warship are always busy running the ship. The crew are divided into watch-keeping teams, which rotate several times a day. Some of the sections on board are able to work at specific times of the day, e.g. in the daytime, or when the operation requires a special effort, at other times of the day. Such sections may include the ship's intelligence section or personnel tasked with maintaining the ship's equipment, sensors etc., but there is always someone on watch, e.g. on the bridge or in the engine control room.

During Operation RECSYR, our operational tasks included escorting and protecting the cargo ships, being constantly ready to handle incidents on the cargo ships, such as fire or damage of some kind, collecting chemical weapons, ensuring the logistics of the cargo ships and solving patrol and intelligence tasks in the operation area.

In addition, we conducted regular training exercises on board the individual ships or internally in the force to build or maintain a high operational level. These training exercises were often combined with patrols in the operation area, focussing especially on the continued protection of the cargo ships.

The ship's daily routine – its so-called 'battle rhythm' – was more or less as follows:

Early morning

- Tactical update in the command centre
- Helicopter briefing – ready for planned or upcoming flights
- Crew briefing
- Mission briefing on the upcoming collection of chemical agents in Syria, where relevant

Beginning of the daily rhythm

- Operations continue with escort and protection of the cargo ships and, where relevant, the collection of chemical agents
- Where relevant, providing the cargo ships with fresh supplies such as food, spare parts and other items to be transferred from the warships
- Internal training on board the warship and joint training in the force

Evening

- Daily progress report is forwarded to the Danish force commander in the operation area
- Daily progress report is forwarded to the Naval Command in Denmark
- Command Team briefing is conducted – the management and key members of staff are briefed of the current and expected future situation in the operation area
- Mission debriefing and mission-specific reporting in the event of a collection of chemical agents

Back home in Denmark, positive dialogue with the Arab media was a main priority, and on 29 December we were therefore joined by a camera crew from the Arab TV network Al Jazeera. I did a live interview for the channel's Arab, American and British viewers – potentially up to 120 million viewers. This was not exactly within my comfort zone, but it was a necessary exercise. Fortunately, things went well, and the reporter did

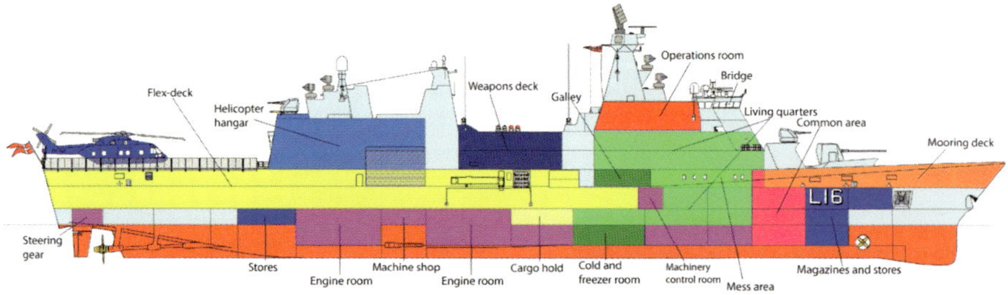

Ship diagram of the Absalon class. The yellow area represents the large leeward deck called the flex deck.

not ask overly critical questions. The most critical question concerned potential pollution of the sea. All I could say was that we had prepared to the best extent possible by providing the cargo ships loaded with chemical agents with as safe an escort as possible.

I spent the rest of the day in meetings with the staff. Here the advantage of the support ship became clear, as the ship's very large leeward deck was equipped with a series of containers with staff facilities where we could comfortably conduct meetings, ensuring easy communication with the rest of the force and the outside world. Among other things, I did an encrypted video conference with the commander of *Helge Ingstad* here, which offered great flexibility with regard to solving the task at hand.

30 December 2013

The day began with the usual morning meeting in the briefing room. I am briefed of any changes to the situation since the meeting the previous evening and the plans for the day in case of specific events of which I need to be aware. My directives this morning included a wish to talk to the crews of the naval force tomorrow – if possible, on board their own units, but as a joint briefing. I encourage the chief of staff to provide suggestions for the content of this briefing. As the Norwegian cargo ship has anchored, I will draw up a letter for them. Similarly, I want to plan a meeting between myself and the commanders of the two warships, the purpose being to go over the Moscow Plan. This must take place as soon as possible after arriving in Limassol tomorrow.

Finally, I asked for the Naval Command to be informed of the maritime situation here in the eastern Mediterranean. This outline of the situation is a summary of the information we receive from our own sensors and other allies. On screen displays, the Russian units appeared as hostile, which I did not consider conducive to our future cooperation, to put it mildly.

Otherwise, we spent the day with exercises, going over our procedures for handling a chemical spill on one of the cargo ships and treatment of the wounded.

According to the original agreement between the Syrian Government and the UN/OPCW, the chemical agents had to leave Syria on 31 December 2013 at the latest. Already in mid-December, it became clear to us that we would not be able to meet this deadline, and by the end of the year not a single container had left Latakia. Instead, we had spent the time training, making sure that we were ready once we received a green light from the OPCW.

At the end of December, I chose to direct the ships towards the holding area two nautical miles out from Syrian territorial waters, where we would join the cargo ships and wait for shipments. I did this intentionally and had received a green light from Moscow to do so. A part of the plan was that we were to be present in the waters off Cyprus and/or in the holding area, ready to collect the first shipment. Furthermore, in my letter to Russia, China and Syria I had informed them that I would be moving my ships to this area. I therefore felt that I had to follow through on what I had communicated.

The reporters who visited us on board *Esbern Snare* were rather disappointed to see that all we did was practise, and that we so far had not collected any chemical agents from Latakia. Their disappointment was

Speaking to the crew on Helge Ingstad.

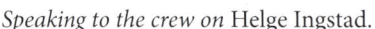

As no shipments with chemical agents had been collected by the end of December 2013, the press had to make do with an interview. In the last days of the month, I contributed to features for the Danish TV stations DR and TV2, as well as the BBC, who sent a camera crew all the way to Limassol. Throughout the operation, I maintained a positive approach to the press – we were after all doing something good here. This open approach involved a risk that the press might 'expose' us, e.g. by announcing when we expected to arrive in Latakia, but it was a risk we had to accept – and if such an announcement were to transpire, we would simply have to increase the level of security. These were the conditions under which we had to operate. If we lost the element of surprise – one of the 10 principles of war – I would simply have to compensate with flexibility, concentration of force and sustainability – three other principles of war.

apparent when we once again called at Limassol at the end of December, and we did not have the heart to tell them that this development did not come as a surprise to us. We returned to Cyprus to celebrate the New Year in port, something the crews had requested, and something I was happy to be able to grant them.

On New Year's Day 31 December, I visited each of the four ships to speak to the crews. I informed them of my view of the immediate future and commended their good work so far and their very professional handling of the situation's uncertainty. Finally, I wished everyone a Happy

New Year. Afterwards, at 17:45, I went to the officer's mess on *Esbern Snare* for New Year's dinner. A part of the splendid meal we enjoyed for the occasion had been cooked by the ship's officers who had volunteered to help out in the galley. And so they had helped one of the cooks prepare part of the meal. Unfortunately, I had not had time to join them myself, but I could tell that it had been a fun and, not least, instructive experience – and the food was delicious.

In keeping with tradition, we then watched the Queen give her New Year's address on TV, before heading to the New Year's festivities in the hangar, which had been set up with lounge music, red lights, beer etc.

Shortly before the festivities began, I met with the commanders. The purpose of this meeting was really to discuss an operational element, but I also used the occasion to stress that we were in a situation where even the smallest mistake could have major and possibly strategic consequences. If, for example, some of the crew members committed a faux pas in town that night, newspaper headlines like 'Danish soldiers sent to transport dangerous warfare agents out of Syria have laid waste to hotel in Cyprus' could cause a lot of damage and, at worst, undermine the political support for the operation. Naturally, this was something I wanted to avoid at all costs, and I therefore asked my commanders to impress on their staff not to let the festivities get out of hand.

Everything went well, and it is my impression that everyone had a good time. I touched glasses with as many as possible and wished everyone a happy New Year at midnight (local time) – 23:00 Danish time – before going to my cabin to call my family. After also having wished my wife and children back home a Happy New Year, I went to bed, and that was the end of 2013.

When in port, I had asked my units to send me a status update each morning on any relevant events having transpired during the night. When I received the morning report on 1 January 2014, I was eager to learn how the evening had gone. And to my great relief, the staff officer on watch could inform me that none of the four ships had anything to report. Well done. The commanders and crews could be proud of themselves.

On the whole, the first day of 2014 was one of the more eventless by far. As was normal for operations of this character, I had a military lawyer among my staff, whose role was to advise me on the legal aspects of

Anordning om forholdsordre for det militære forsvar ved angreb på landet og under krig.

Vi Frederik den Niende, af Guds Nåde Konge til Danmark, de Venders og Goters,
Hertug til Slesvig, Holsten, Stormarn, Ditmarsken, Lauenborg og Oldenborg,

Gør vitterligt:

I tilfælde af angreb på dansk territorium eller på dansk militær enhed uden for dansk territorium skal de angrebne styrker ufortøvet optage kampen uden at ordre afventes eller søges indhentet, selv om krigserklæring eller krigstilstand ikke er de pågældende chefer bekendt.

Dersom forsvarets styrker ikke inden angrebet er bragt op på fuld krigsstyrke, er ethvert angreb på Danmark ude fra eller på dets forfatningsmæssige myndigheder at betragte som ordre til mobilisering.

Hjemmeværnet møder uopholdeligt som bestemt ved „Hjemmeværnet på plads".

Der må forventes ved krigsudbrud og under krigstilstand at ville fremkomme falske ordrer og meddelelser til befolkningen og til mobiliserende eller kæmpende styrker.

Ordrer om ikke at mobilisere eller ikke at gøre modstand eller afbryde påbegyndt mobilisering eller kamp må derfor ikke adlydes, før der foreligger fornøden vished for, at ordren er udstedt af dertil kompetent myndighed.

Ordrer fra forfatningsmæssige myndigheder, der er taget til fange, eller som af fjenden er sat ud af funktion på anden måde, skal ikke adlydes.

Angrebne enheder eller enheder i nærheden af angrebne enheder sætter uden at afvente ordre omgående alle til rådighed stående midler ind i kampen. Isolerede styrker skal, under energiske forsøg på at sinke fjendens fremrykning mest muligt og tilføje ham størst mulige tab, søge forbindelse med andre kæmpende danske eller allierede enheder.

Kampen skal, selv om styrkerne kæmper isoleret, føres med største energi for herved at skaffe tid til at organisere styrker i eller uden for området.

Kampen skal fortsættes, selv om fjenden truer med repressalier for at bevæge vore styrker til overgivelse. Bliver det uomgængelig nødvendigt at opgive et landområde til fjenden, skal styrkerne gøre, hvad der er muligt for at nå frem til forsvarskampen på andre frontafsnit.

Chefer for landsdelskommandoer, regioner, regimenter, selvstændige afdelinger, marinekommandoer, -distrikter, basiskommandoer m. fl. træffer, når angreb er erkendt, alle foranstaltninger til at forøge deres enheders fredsstyrke i overensstemmelse med de gældende bestemmelser, og søger snarest kampen vendt fra forsvar til angreb.

5. kolonnevirksomhed skal bekæmpes. Politiet vil på dette område bistå de militære myndigheder.

Våben og andet krigsmateriel må aldrig falde i fjendens hånd i brugbar stand.

Befalingsmænd, mather og værnepligtige af hær, søværn, flyvevåben, korps m. fl., — hvadenten de er tjenstgørende, afskedigede (endnu mødepligtige ved mobilisering), hjemkommanderede eller hjemsendte — skal, når angreb på Danmark erfares, ufortøvet og uden at afvente ordre om mobilisering give møde som befalet ved designeringsskrivelse eller på den i soldaterbogen (orlogsbogen) indklæbede røde mødebefaling.

Såfremt landet bliver delvis besat af angriberen, skal alle, der ikke kan nå frem til deres egen afdeling, tilslutte sig andre kæmpende danske eller allierede enheder.

Af det personel af værnene, der er overført til hjemmeværnet, skal de, der i fredstid er iklædt og udrustet, møde som bestemt ved „Hjemmeværnet på plads". Det øvrige personel af værnene, der er overført til hjemmeværnet, skal derimod afvente nærmere ordre.

Givet på Amalienborg, den 6. marts 1952.

Under Vor Kongelige Hånd og Segl.

Frederik R.

(L. S.)

Harald Petersen.

Fo 43-124

'Danish Royal Decree No. 63 of 6 march 1952 concerning Rules of Engagement for the Armed Forces in Case of an Attack on the Country and in Time of War', also known as the 'Royal Decree'. The decree describes how Danish military forces are to act in case of an attack on the force or the country with no previous declaration of war.

the operation. We spent a great part of the day going over the force's so-called Rules of Engagement, describing when it is legally acceptable to use force to achieve an objective or to protect units or personnel. These were not the most complex set of rules, as we simply operated under the international right to self-defence and the Danish Royal Decree. This meant that we were authorised to open fire in the event of an attack on the ship or on units under our protection.

Even though we were part of the same force, the Danish and Norwegian units did not operate under the same Rules of Engagement. For instance, I was free to decide whether the mission required us to enter Syrian territorial waters, whereas the Norwegians first had to ask permission from the supreme command of the Norwegian Navy back home in Norway. In practice, this was not a problem, though, as we were able to plan operations in Syrian waters in good time, giving *Helge Ingstad* and *Taiko* time to obtain the necessary permissions.

That evening we received a call from the Chinese embassy in Cyprus. The Chinese frigate *Yancheng*, which was on its way to the waters off Syria, had now reached the Red Sea, and the ambassador therefore wanted to start planning our communication and cooperation with the representatives of the Chinese Navy. I was well-disposed towards this cooperation and suggested that we should not just exchange contact information but also conduct joint exercises along with the Russian units in the area. I therefore chose to invite the commanders of the Chinese frigate and the Russian cruiser on board *Esbern Snare* on 6 January to meet in person and explore the possibility of conducting joint exercises.

At the same time, I received a message from the UN saying that the date of the first pickup of chemical agents in Latakia seemed to be approaching. Of course, we were ready to get to work, so this was good news.

2 January 2014
The day began when I woke at around 8:30. This meant that I had gotten eight hours of sleep. It is the first time I've slept for so long since arriving, and it was great. I had brunch, which is something we have when we are in port.

At 10:00 I had a meeting with the staff, where the chief of staff, the principal warfare officer and I went over the fragmentary order they had produced for this part of the operation, from the time we enter Syrian waters and leave again. I have asked them to describe this in detail to make sure there are no loose ends. Unfortunately, this does not leave the commanders a high degree of freedom to manoeuvre, but it is important for me to have this part of the operation under complete control. Yesterday, when I read the fragmentary order, I had a few comments. They considered my comments this morning, and now they wish to discuss them with me. In between, we had the usual morning staff meeting, which is at 11:00 when we are in port, and at 08:00 when we are at sea. Nothing new really at this meeting.

We then continued work on the fragmentary order, also called a FRAGO, until the commanders' meeting at 12:30, where we would be discussing the FRAGO. I went over the details of the order with the commanders, giving them a chance to ask questions and make suggestions for changes and ensuring that they had full knowledge of its content. It went well.

Afterwards I informed them of my decision with regard to the loading plans. I had decided that *Taiko* would receive 117 containers holding second-priority agents and 24 containing first-priority agents. *Ark Futura* would carry 133 containers with first-priority agents. Once the cargo had been loaded onto the cargo ships, they would meet with *Cape Ray*, and the first-priority agents would undergo hydrolysis to transform them into second-priority agents, which we then expected to transport to a facility for final destruction in either Germany, Finland, the US or Great Britain.

I told the commanders today, because I now have sufficient knowledge of the unloading process and other aspects, to plan for dividing the cargo between the two cargo ships. You would not believe the scale of politics in this operation. It is almost as if Norway and Denmark are competing to be the first to enter the port and carry the most dangerous agents. The one who comes first carrying the most hazardous substance wins!

With regard to the division of substances, I have considered the size of the cargo ships; with regard to the ports they must enter in connection with their destruction, and their equipment – cranes, hatches, etc. Also, and just as importantly, I have tried to group the individual agents depending on the danger if they are allowed to mix in the event of a spill. After all, the cargo will contain the ingredients for chemical warfare agents, and there is no reason to load all the ingredients for nerve gas, for example, onto the same ship if this can be prevented.

The result of this overall balancing act is that the Danish cargo ship will be the first to leave the port, carrying the most dangerous agents, even though this may prove a challenge to Norway, which, to my knowledge, pays a lot of money each day to rent a cargo ship, which will then have to wait to participate. We will see what happens, but we have to use the ships available to us, with their advantages and disadvantages, and it is my job to come up with a plan that supports the actual conditions as well as possible, and that's that.

After the meeting, I presented the rules for the use of force (the Rules of Engagement), and I have just applied the finishing touches to an order concerning these rules, which will be announced today.

I then left for the Norwegian frigate to talk to four different media outlets who wanted to know what had caused the delay, and when we would be making the first pickup, which they wanted to make slightly dramatic. They were disappointed when all I could say was that we would sail out in the morning as per our routine to practise and train, and if we are called upon, we will head out. I am starting to get used to this press circus.

Then back to the ship, where I have spent the evening working by the computer. There are a lot of signals and communication to approve and a lot of problems with my ship-to-ship meeting scheduled for 6 January. A lot of well-meaning, but not very helpful officers back home constantly cause trouble, e.g. by informing China that we will be in the port of Limassol on 5 January. We will not! It would make my job a lot easier if only people would stick to what they know for certain. Of course, they mean well, but it is a hassle for me to clear up, and the Chinese will act on information they receive from diplomatic channels. Is it too much to ask to confer with someone who knows the answer before writing to China and Russia?

Oh, well. It is now 00:30, and I am about to turn in. We sail at 06:00, and the wakeup call is at 05:45, so to bed, to bed.

3 January 2014

Today we put out to sea again. I do like it best when we are at sea. Things calm down, and there is a better rhythm on board than in port. We left early, at 06:00, so I had to get up at 05:30, and then you might as well set to work. The usual morning meeting was at 08:00, where the officer on watch informs me of events since the previous evening. As we had been in port, fortunately, there was little to report. The main aim of the meeting this morning was to identify the location of the Chinese frigate. N2 (the Intelligence Section) could enlighten us: They had learned that it had just left the Suez. This was consistent with indications saying that it would arrive today. And a few hours later the officer on watch heard that it was on its way, when it communicated with the Norwegian frigate over the radio.

I spent the morning describing the pickup plan. I was rather worried about announcing it without conferring with more people. I therefore asked the chemist and representative of the Danish Emergency Management Agency to take a look at it. This resulted in a couple of minor changes, before I decided to forward it.

I also gave an interview today to the Associated Press, which has made a three-minute feature available on their website. I have not seen it yet, but my press officer tells me that it's good. Also, I have answered questions presented by three Danish media outlets. We will see what comes out of this. They will probably print something more sensational than my presentation of events.

This afternoon the Organization for the Prohibition of Chemical Weapons (OPCW) realised that there is such a thing as reporters, and now they are suddenly too dangerous to have on board.

All I have to say to that is that they are too late. They are on board, we are at sea, and if we limit them in their work, the case will turn sour. The OPCW argues that it is a matter of safety, but that is not true, because everyone will know where we are at all times. We will be using civilian channels to call and communicate with the Chinese and Russian units, and we have to announce our arrival before calling at Latakia, who will send a pilot and tugboats to meet us, so our presence will be known, regardless of whether the press is here or not. The real problem is if the OPCW announces the arrival of a shipment, and we receive a report when we are on our way saying that the shipment has not arrived after all, giving the OPCW a hard time explaining why. After all, the international community is pushing for the job to be done as soon as possible.

Well, the OPCW managed to scare the Danish Ministry of Defence, so now we are waiting for a new policy from Defence Command Denmark concerning the press, and then we will just have to wait and see whether I have to throw the reporters off the ship. I discussed the matter with the Chief of the Naval Command, and I told him that of course I should not be blamed for making myself available for interviews time and again; I do so because Denmark and thus also the Danish Ministry of Defence – at least up until now – wanted to pursue an outward-oriented policy in this area. All I have to say then is that it might look stupid, but of course I will do what they want me to – which is what I have been doing all along.

This evening the intelligence team reported that the opposition, as a response to the regime's decision to throw bombs made of oil barrels containing explosives from e.g. helicopters at Aleppo, planned to launch reprisal attacks in the suburbs of Latakia. This made me ask the units to identify the measures available to them in the event of indirect fire, such as mortars and rockets etc. Even though we probably will not represent a target, we must not rule out situations where a stray rocket or mortar falls wide and instead lands close to us.

And so, this evening I realised that the thinking back home is that I, at my level, am meant to handle the entire press policy. Why, I should be able to handle the aspect of strategic communication with Russia and China at the tactical meeting scheduled for 6 January. My answer to that is: No. I cannot. The press aspect – it is so politically charged that they will have to manage that without my help at the strategic level. What I do is tactics and thus policy implementation, including press policy implementation, but they are solely responsible for the overall strategy in the area. Now, I hope they will live up to that responsibility.

Over the next few days, the presence of the press on board the ship developed into an issue between myself, the OPCW and the Danish Ministry of Foreign Affairs as well as the Danish Ministry of Defence back home. The latter three feared that the reporters on board would accidentally compromise our safety and thus jeopardise the entire mission. In my opinion, both the OPCW and the Danish authorities preferred to see the reporters leave the ship or be prevented from transmitting. At the same time, though, it was clear to me that none of them wanted to take responsibility for such a decision. The OPCW's proposal mostly consisted of general and useless statements, really, and so I had to reply that their guidelines were too general. After all, I was not meant to be involved in drawing up the policies; my job was to implement the policies that had been decided at the levels above me.

As early as late November 2013, I had asked the OPCW mission headquarters in Cyprus to draw up a comprehensive press policy. Their answer had been that the OPCW did not want to take steps in that direction, and that such a policy was the responsibility of the participating nations. I had disagreed, as I felt that the press – like all other aspects of such an operation – had to be controlled to reach the optimal effect. The OPCW could not be persuaded to change their minds, however, which meant that we on *Esbern Snare* and the Norwegians on *Helge Ingstad* had chosen to pursue a very open press policy, as we considered the entire mission a good and positive story. The OPCW now wanted us to reverse that decision, and I disagreed. So far, my answer to the OPCW was that the issue had been tabled, but this did not settle the matter.

On 4 January, I was informed that Russia and China had accepted my invitation to a tactical ship-to-ship meeting on 6 January. Unfortunately, this only constituted a partial victory, as Russia was 'unfortunately unable to participate' with crew from *Pyotr Velikiy*, but would send the Russian defence attaché in Cyprus. Of course, the Russians could have sent officers from *Pyotr Velikiy* had they wanted to, and the decision was more likely based on a wish among the Russian establishment in Moscow not to give me an opportunity to discuss the operation in person with the commander of the cruiser just yet. Perhaps he had yet to have been informed of the plan. Imagine if he and I together decided to change the plan drawn up in Moscow!

I found the decision frustrating, but I could not do anything to change it, and I chose to go through with the meeting nonetheless. The Chinese had already emailed me to say that they would be happy to attend, and all we could do was send the minutes of the meeting to *Pyotr Velikiy* if we made any decisions that affected them. So, while I was slightly

The Chinese frigate Huangshan, *which replaced* Yancheng *in the spring of 2014 is here seen in the waters off Syria. The modern frigates had a displacement of approx. 4,000 tons, a maximum speed of 27 knots and a crew of approx. 165. At the time of writing, the Chinese Navy has at its disposal 28 units of this type. In the background is the Russian destroyer* Vice-Admiral Kulakov *of the Udaloy class, which replaced* Pyotr Velikiy *in the mission area in April 2014.*

disappointed with the Russians, my first impression of the Chinese was positive. They spoke English very well and were very easy to talk to, which gave me high hopes for our cooperation.

January 4th was also the day we were informed that the Syrians were ready for us to pick up the first shipment of chemical agents in Latakia. The pickup was scheduled for the afternoon/evening of 7 January and would involve a shipment of so-called B salt – one of three ingredients required to produce sarin nerve gas. The date suited us well, also in the light of our meeting with the Chinese and Russians on 6 January, and we were happy finally to see the operation begin. At the same time, though, it became clear to us that the threat against Latakia had increased in the last few weeks of December and the beginning of January. Among other things, the rebel forces had fired rockets into the city on several occasions. These attacks had focussed on the suburbs, which were relatively far away from the port, and the risk of being attacked and hit was therefore minor. Still, a stray rocket might strike close enough to one of our

The view from the bridge on Esbern Snare *across the port of Latakia. Inside the port is* Ark Futura. *(R.R. Nicolaisen)*

ships to injure the crew or damage the ship, not to mention our personnel in the port itself, which included the staff operating the mobile scanner. I therefore used the opportunity to ask the units to identify procedures that could be introduced to minimise the risk of the personnel positioned on the deck, the bridge or in similarly exposed positions.

It was my impression that the rebel forces usually fired a smaller number of rockets during an attack, and I thus decided that unless rockets struck the part of the port where we would be picking up the shipment, I would allow the mission to continue. I was convinced that the rebel forces would not fire at us intentionally, as such an attack would undermine the foreign support on which the rebels depended so very much. But we knew that their inaccurate rockets could nevertheless become a problem. I had seen something similar in Iraq, where I on previous postings for Defence Command Denmark had experienced attacks on Camp Bastion on several occasions. I knew how these rockets are usually fired – namely by placing them inside a drainpipe, which is pointed towards the desired target, and then the rocket is fired using a simple striker. Thus, as a weapon, they are neither particularly sophisticated nor very accurate.

We therefore drew up a plan for moving *Ark Future* and/or *Taiko* out of the port of Latakia quickly if we came under fire. The warships would then be positioned outside the port to enable them to defend the cargo ships more effectively than if we were tied to the pier or had to manoeuvre inside the port. At sea we would enjoy greater freedom of movement, and because the piers in Latakia were low, we would be able to oversee the entire port and most of the city of Latakia from the bridge of *Esbern Snare*. Moreover, we would be able to move around to ensure that as many of our weapons as possible could reach a potential target by firing across the docks if necessary.

So, even though I still hoped and expected to be able to complete the task by drawing on the 'diplomat' only, the 'warrior' in me was always ready to step up if necessary.

On 5 January the OPCW told us to drop off the reporters on board *Esbern Snare* and *Helge Ingstad* before sailing to Latakia. The Syrian authorities had pressured the OPCW into making this decision. The Syrian authorities would not accept the presence of reporters on board ships participating in the operation, and as the OPCW did not want to give the Syrians an excuse to call off or postpone the pickup, they yielded. The official grounds for the Syrian decision were security concerns, but a main factor was really that the Syrian Government did not consider the handover of chemical agents a cause for celebration or something that should be reported by the press or others for that matter. They considered the handover the lesser of two evils, and this meant that we had to drop off the various press teams in Limassol the next day.

Due to safety considerations, we still had not told anyone on board that we would be collecting the first shipment of chemical agents in Latakia on 7 January. It was difficult to keep it secret though, as everyone on board was anxious to get started and therefore wanted to be informed of any progress. Yet at the same time, I knew that a lot could still go wrong, and I did not want to tell them that we were leaving only to have to tell them later that this was not the case after all. That the situation was untenable became clear to me the evening of 5 January, when we realised that the authorities in Latakia had not been informed of the agreement reached at the meeting in Moscow on 27 December. They therefore expected me to follow the Russian plan, which among other things involved letting our warships wait just outside Syrian territorial waters while the cargo ships collected the chemical agents in the port. Nevertheless, I intended to follow the Moscow Plan, as agreed. To the letter.

To be honest, it was frustrating to have to cooperate with these centralised forces who did not know anything and, which is far worse, did not dare to do anything unless the order came from Moscow, Beijing or Damascus. Nonetheless, I maintained that we should stick one hundred per cent to the Moscow Plan, regardless of whether the local authorities in Latakia considered it appropriate or not. The plan had been approved by all the parties involved, and it would therefore constitute the guiding principle of Operation RECSYR.

The day ended with a staff meeting focussing on the last preparations before the tactical meeting, which would take place the following morning. The meeting ran late, because the staff had drawn up a rather ambitious plan for our cooperation with the Chinese, and I was not completely sure that it was realistic. Both because I wanted to keep our new partners at arm's length, seeing as they did not share our Western view of the Syrian civil war, and because I was not sure that they were in fact prepared for anything but very simple procedures and very simple communication. Neither the Russians nor the Chinese were familiar with our procedures, and based on previous experience I expected them to be very reluctant to agree to any kind of cooperation for fear of what their superiors in Moscow and Beijing would say to such a step.

6 January 2014

At 10:00 the Chinese delegation arrived, comprising Deputy Commander of the Chinese force (called ETG 546), Senior Captain Li Xiaodong, Commander of *Yancheng*, Captain Zhang, and the force's Operations Officer, Captain Sun Hongyu. Russia was represented by the Russian defence attaché in Cyprus. We went to the staff rooms, where I intended to brief them of the plan we had drawn up yesterday. This would require a lot of energy and patience. Speaking slowly and waiting for the translation into Chinese, speaking slowly and waiting for the translation into Chinese etc.

Seeing as the Russians had chosen to send the Russian defence attaché (the reason why they had not sent the commander of the cruiser was that it was supposedly several days away. Odd, as we had it plotted nearby), naturally he could not really contribute, only report back to Moscow! Well, I knew that this would be the case. Have experienced something similar a couple of times now.

When the meeting began, I tried to establish eye contact with the Chinese, but they were very stone-faced. Not even a smile, and very little interaction. Things improved a bit later on, but it was anything but a dynamic meeting. It also became clear to me that there had been no coordination at all between Russia and China. I knew that we would be collecting the first shipment the following day, but the Chinese had not been informed, and it was not my place to tell them. This had to be done at the level above me.

At the meeting, we discussed simple tactical elements such as code words for the various stages of the Moscow Plan, communication frequencies, reference points etc., but due to the lack of participation from *Pyotr Velikiy*, we did not touch on the more detailed coordination of the two forces' operations. The Russian defence attaché left the meeting with the briefing, which he could then forward to *Pyotr Velikiy* via Moscow. We also informed them that the slightly more detailed aspects of the briefing and the further operationalisation of the Moscow Plan of course did not apply, but that they could study the briefing until we got a new chance to meet with all the seagoing parties. It was crucial for me to ensure that the Russians did not consider the meeting a fait accompli; they should of course also be heard/able to provide input, just like the other participants.

The journal continues:
I am also not sure that the Chinese delegation in fact has anything to do with maritime operations. I am pretty sure that at least one of them was from the Chinese military intelligence services, but of course that is also part of the game. This became obvious during lunch, when he suddenly asked the commander of *Helge Ingstad* how many aerial targets his radar could keep track of at a time. The

Norwegian frigate is equipped with a very sophisticated US-produced radar that is capable of tracking many targets simultaneously. The commander wisely responded, 'More than a few', and that was the end of that conversation. ☺

This afternoon I had to have a difficult talk with the two reporters on board. They were given an hour to pack, before they were sailed into Limassol. Naturally, there was little else to do than to inform them that it had been decided that we could not continue to accommodate the press.

But the reporters were very professional, though surprised of course, and not least afraid that it was because they had done something wrong. I assured them that this was not the case. I got my press officer to collect the email addresses of their superiors, and I have sent them a nice email explaining that the decision to drop them off had nothing to do with them.

Unfortunately, I did not manage to get to bed before late tonight, as there were a lot of things to do before the first pickup. I find it unbelievable that some of the papers still have not been signed by the sender, Syria, and the recipient, Finland, a few hours before departure. Everything should have been settled, as my staff includes Finnish chemical specialists, and they should also be allowed to enter Syria legally. Well, I managed to get that done, just as I have corrected an error made by the Naval Command, as the Danish OPCW liaison officer in Cyprus had asked Great Britain to confirm the name of the port receiving the first shipment, which at a later point in time will be sent to Great Britain for destruction. Why on earth should Great Britain, long before the shipment is set to arrive, decide on an exact port? There is no reason to pressure them into making an official announcement at this point, as they may for domestic political reasons have cause not to announce the name of the port until the last minute. The word 'exact' is then forwarded to the Danish Ministry of Defence and the Danish Ministry of Foreign Affairs, and then all hell breaks loose because Great Britain still – and very understandably – does not want to make such an announcement. At midnight, I then received permission from the Chief of Defence to collect the first shipment.

Another reason why I had to work until late today was that the Chinese had suddenly realised that we were heading northeast, even though I had in fact informed them of this the previous day. The Chinese frigate was still at Limassol, and they called us to ask what we were doing, and if we knew anything about the first shipment. They asked to talk to Commodore Mikkelsen, but I sent my chief of staff to answer the phone. Afterwards he came down to tell me that he had told them what I had already told them – that we were merely going to the holding area to be ready in case something happened – but nothing about a shipment, and that they had to ask the OPCW. I had told him to say that because I did not want to drive a wedge between China and Russia by keeping the Chinese unit informed, if it turns out that Russia does not want them to participate in the first pickup. I do not know whether that is the case at all, but it is a game I would rather not get involved in, and it could easily make them consider me the opposite of an 'equal partner', namely the one who wants to coordinate events, make the decisions and take control.

Nonetheless, they kept calling and sounded almost despairing in the end. The Russians did not tell them anything, and I knew that the Russians were following us to Latakia. In the end – after midnight and thus on the day of the pickup – I took pity on them. After all, they had called several times, but now insisted on talking to me in person. I chose to tell them everything, including that we would meet at the agreed location at 07:30 and then sail towards Latakia for the pickup. I also promised to send them an email with more details. They were very surprised to hear this, as there were just seven and a half hours to the meeting time, and it would take them 10-11 hours at 15 knots to get there from Limassol. I told them out of consideration for the grand strategic interests. Because it was not a question of whether the Chinese frigate would participate in the first collection of chemical agents from Syria, but of whether the People's Republic of China would participate in the first collection of chemical agents from Syria. I risked potential complaints from the Russians. What was vital to me was the overall picture.

***

The First Pickup

7 January 2014

Ark Futura *sailing towards Latakia on 7 January 2014 for the first pickup of chemical agents. According to plan, we would enter Latakia several times to collect chemical agents. In the meantime,* Ark Futura *and* Taiko *would wait in the holding area outside the Syrian port, where the ships and their cargo of chemical weapons and agents could be protected against attacks from Syrian rebel forces or terrorists. Therefore, each of the two cargo ships was equipped with a Vessel Protection Team for active defence, comprising members of the Danish Frogman Corps and the Norwegian Coastal Rangers, respectively.*

The day of the first pickup in Latakia is here. A slightly restless night. Got to bed late and had had too much coffee. Also excited – after all, this is our first time in Syria, and we still have a number of unresolved questions, which we will have to handle in the process. Rose early and went to the staff room, where I was told that the lorries were still at Homs and had not begun to move towards Latakia. What to believe: the GPS trackers on the lorries or the staff in Latakia telling us that they were on their way. We headed towards the port!

The plot told me that our Chinese friends were rushing towards us at 27 knots. Believe they have managed to leave Limassol and get going quickly. Pleased to see that they have made it.

We began to get organised as planned, heading towards the holding point and *Ark Futura*, and prepared to transfer the chemical specialists and staff from the Danish Customs and Tax Administration to *Ark Futura*. We informed *Pyotr Velikiy* that we were approaching and would send the Norwegian frigate to the northern area. This was according to plan, and things were going well. ☺

At one point, when we were in the middle of Syrian territorial waters, I made the officer on watch ask the Russians whether they intended to live up to the Moscow Plan and provide protection of the southern area. He responded that he would send the Chinese frigate. As agreed in the Moscow Plan, I also offered the Russians to transfer a liaison officer to *Pyotr Velikiy*, but they declined.

Shortly afterwards, we could see the Chinese frigate enter the southern area to cover us from the south, as agreed in Moscow. So far, so good. Two nautical miles into Syrian territorial waters, I kept asking about the containers, which had not moved for the past eight hours, as far as I could see, and suddenly Latakia informed us that the containers would not be arriving just yet. We aborted the operation, and as planned all the ships turned around and moved away from the coast.

I decided to stay approx. 14 nautical miles from the coast until I could see the containers move and knew when they would arrive in Latakia. An hour and a half passed. Still no movement. Suddenly we were informed that the first containers would reach the port in an hour. Apparently, the GPS trackers had been set to send a signal once every 24 hours only, but the OPCW had their own trackers on the containers. ☹ What good are GPS trackers in a situation like this if they only update their position once every 24 hours?

We sailed into position again and headed for the coast. Everyone was happy and trusted this to be it. Again, everything went well and according to plan. The OPCW mission headquarters in Latakia had called our liaison officer, Pet Moll, in Cyprus to tell him to call Commodore Mikkelsen and ask him to hurry. Per, cool as he is, had said that he had no intention whatsoever to call the admiral to state the obvious. We would arrive when the tactical situation allowed. Good man. ☺

The bridge on Esbern Snare *at general quarters. Everyone is wearing helmets, flak vests and fire-resistant clothing.*

We were at general quarters with everyone in position, wearing bulletproof vests and helmets on deck and bridge, and ready for whatever was about to happen. On the way in, we were told that the first three containers had arrived. Hallelujah. This was it.

I did not ask about the small issue of our armed dinghies, which we wanted to use on the way in and inside the port. We did everything as had been agreed and communicated in Moscow, even though I had not received official confirmation that we were allowed to use these smaller vessels inside Syrian waters. Everyone agreed to the plan, and things went well. We followed and checked the pilot boat until we were certain that it was in fact the Syrian pilot. This phase can be critical, because it is after all easy for someone with malign intent to grab a boat and pretend to be the pilot. The same goes for tugboats, which also come very close to the cargo ships.

As we approached the port, we could see that a large number of security personnel were present in the port. There were soldiers everywhere, on piers and roofs. There were two Syrian missile vessels in the water, and people were patrolling the port looking for potential bombs. The Syrians wanted to make things as safe as possible. The port had been sealed off, and all cargo ships had been guided away from the anchoring place, which was where *Esbern Snare* would dock shortly, ready to defend and assist, if necessary. On board the warship everything had been planned, down to the smallest detail, and everything went according to plan. This was truly a historic moment and quite incredible.

Everything was peaceful. The buildings in the port seemed to be empty, almost unfinished. Something was burning on the slope north of the port, close to a mosque, and there were a couple of fire engines at the scene, but otherwise all we could see was some smoke coming from a building in the city. And of course, that could be any number of things. Everyone was on their toes and ready – it was momentous.

Soon the scanner and chemical specialists were in position, and we set about examining the containers. In the meantime, we had to do the paperwork. This did not pose any problems, and I felt very positive. Everyone felt that we could do this fast and that we would be able to leave soon. But even though everything was peaceful, the situation nevertheless became more and more dangerous, the longer we stayed. So, the plan is 'fast in and fast out'.

A lorry scan from the Danish Customs and Tax Administration's scanner.

Once the containers had been examined, I was told that Niels Thomsen, Captain of *Ark Futura*, was not fully satisfied with the papers. The authorities back home had informed him that an exact address of delivery was missing, just as the Syrian Government was not to be listed as the sender. I went to the bridge myself, grabbed the radio and called Niels. He had not been told that it was okay to have the Syrian Government listed as sender. The problem is, and it is something I have been trying to solve right from the start, that standard civilian procedures from e.g. container management in the Danish port of Esbjerg have been expected to apply here in Syria as well, in spite of procedures down here being very different.

Fortunately, Niels is a pragmatic person, so he had begun loading containers onto the ship, and I thought everything went well. After a short while I was told that the containers had been unloaded again because our military logistics manager (back home in Denmark) had called Niels and reversed our joint decision to load the containers, because he – sitting in Denmark – did not consider the paperwork to be satisfactory.

To me, this was the last straw. I called the Chief of the Naval Command directly and asked him to deal with it. I did not want to have to wait in the port in Syria for someone back home to find the cargo satisfactory. The person in question knows all there is to know about 'standard' container management, but nothing about the security risk he was exposing crew and ships to by reversing my decision. The matter was quickly settled, and the containers were loaded. This would have consequences!

Everything was good, and we were able to leave Latakia according to plan in the most beautiful sunset imaginable. In many ways, it was a very historic moment. Almost surreal that I would be witnessing it.

Once we had left the port, we just had to leave Syrian territorial waters as fast as possible, settle at a lower stage of readiness and relax for a bit. Great. Now the crew got to do what we had come to do, and what they had trained hard for. To me, this also meant that procedures and plans – except for the paper-pushing back home – had run like clockwork.

Ark Futura leaving Syrian waters in a most beautiful sunset.

A Bomb on Board?

I was pretty tired the day following the first pickup and had really hoped for a quiet day, but things turned out differently. In the morning, it was suggested to us that 'something' might have been placed inside one of the containers. This was not pleasant news, seeing as the containers had already been loaded and we were now waiting in international waters.

A lot of thoughts go through your head when you receive such a message. What were the odds of this happening, as we had scanned the containers before allowing them on board? Had a potential bomb been fitted with a time device or a booby trap to make it detonate in our faces at a given time or during a potential attempt to disarm it? If the device required a mobile phone to activate, then luckily, we were out of range. But if we had to move the containers to a safe location for further inspection, then we might have to move so close to land that we might be within range of a mobile phone. And what about the civilian crew on *Ark Futura*? How ought we deal with the fact that they might be in harm's way? I had to consider these and many other questions.

Three containers on the deck of Ark Futura.

I asked the commander of our team of frogmen to leave *Ark Futura* and meet me on *Esbern Snare*. By virtue of their training, members of the Danish Frogman Corps possess in-depth knowledge on explosives, and the team would be able to assess our options, e.g. with regard to dismantling a potential bomb and, if relevant, the need for external support.

Fortunately, the chemical agents we had collected in Latakia were not the most hazardous of the ones we would be dealing with, so the content of the containers was not my main concern. We also had with us a series of specialists in chemical agents, but this did not change the fact that opening a potentially booby-trapped container on the deck of *Ark Futura* would be a laborious as well as dangerous operation.

We managed to remain calm, not least because we told ourselves that if anyone wanted to get at us, they would probably have tried to attack us while we were close to land and thus could be filmed for television. Now that we were far away from the coast, no one would be able to see an attack, thus reducing its propaganda effect. Seen in this light, I decided to allow the necessary time to try to resolve the situation differently. I needed to apply what we in military contexts refer to as tactical patience. I therefore got in touch with Frank Trojahn to inform him that I would

Chemical agents in a container on board Taiko.

not be reporting this incident officially to anyone back home, but only tell him over the phone. The reason for this was simply that if I began to send home signals about the incident, it was likely to generate unnecessary – though well-intentioned – involvement at the strategic level and provoke a panic. As the person in charge at the scene, I had full knowledge of the situation and was the right person to make the necessary decisions, and my request for tactical patience was therefore granted.

I asked the captain of *Ark Futura* to join me on *Esbern Snare*, and I informed him of the situation and our thoughts on the matter. He should be prepared if anything did happen on board. He was clearly surprised, but I managed to set his mind at rest. I told him that if I had considered the situation to be dangerous, then we naturally would not be sitting here, chatting about it over a cup of coffee. It was my firm belief that the suspicion did not have any basis in reality, but this did not change the fact that we had to look into the matter one way or another.

I cannot reveal how we resolved the situation, but late that evening we were able to conclude that 'nothing' had been placed inside one of the containers, and we therefore did not have to open them to carry out a visual inspection. This was good news, which I immediately passed on to the captain of *Ark Futura*. If we had been forced to open one or more of the containers and thus break the OPCW seal, it could have caused trouble in connection with the next shipment of chemical agents; fortunately, we avoided such a situation.

That evening the commander of *Esbern Snare* asked me whether *Esbern Snare* and *Ark Futura* were allowed to head towards Larnaca in Cyprus. A family member of one of the crew members on *Esbern Snare* had died, and he was therefore anxious to return home. This is the kind of request you as a superior officer do your utmost to meet, and as no pickup had been planned for the next couple of days, we were able to sail close enough to Cyprus that the helicopter on board *Esbern Snare* could take the deckhand into Larnaca.

And that was the end of that day, which did not turn out as quiet as I had hoped, to say the least.

On 9 January, the Lynx helicopter on Esbern Snare *– called Blue Ghost – flew the deckhand to Larnaca in Cyprus from where he could continue his journey home.*

A Russian Coup Attempt

The events on 7 January, where our cooperation with the Russian and Chinese ships had not gone exactly as planned, prompted me to call a new coordination meeting between the commanders of *Pyotr Velikiy*, the Chinese frigate and myself. Just like the first meeting, it would take place on board *Esbern Snare* and was scheduled for 10 January. I planned for the meeting to be more or less a copy of the meeting on 6 January, and at the meeting we would revisit the tactical details from the previous meeting and incorporate our experiences from the pickup on 7 January. However, the Russians were of a different opinion, which put my internal 'diplomat' to the test.

The meeting was set to last two hours, and unlike the first meeting, the commander of *Pyotr Velikiy*, Commodore Oleg Peshkurov, chose (or was allowed) to participate in this meeting. At the beginning of the meeting the Russians informed us that they had also prepared a briefing and a proposal for a joint effort. This came as a surprise, because a plan had already been made in Moscow, but naturally they were allowed to present this new plan. As planned, I opened the meeting with my briefing, which was basically a repetition of the one the Chinese had received on 6 January. And my presentation did not prompt a lot of comments from neither the Russians nor the Chinese, both of whom were clearly waiting for the presentation of the Russian plan. Before we moved on to that point on the agenda, we took a ten-minute break, as the Russians wanted to go out for a smoke. Even though I do not smoke, I joined them on deck and managed to chat with them, getting them to loosen up a bit.

After the break, the commander of *Pyotr Velikiy* presented the Russian plan. Fortunately, as the briefing had been downloaded to our computer during the break, I had managed to sneak a peek of what they wanted to say, so I was prepared when they informed us that they wanted to be in charge of coordinating the positions of the participating ships from now on, including the Danish/Norwegian ships in my force. They substantiated this request based on dissatisfaction with the fact that we operated with two virtually identical coordination structures. The Russians felt that this was problematic and instead wanted to operate as one unified force. According to the Russian self-understanding, however, this meant that the coordination unit should be on board *Pyotr Velikiy*. The commander of the cruiser therefore said that they hoped that Denmark, Norway, China and possibly Syria at the earliest possible opportunity would transfer a liaison officer to the Russian flagship to establish this unified (and Russian-controlled) command structure.

The Russians did not present the plan as a proposal for discussion, but neither did they get very far in their presentation before I asked them whether they would take comments now or preferred to wait until afterwards. When they said that I was welcome to comment now, I immediately pointed out that I considered the Russian commander and myself to be equal force commanders and that I therefore would not be subject to their directives. According to the Moscow Plan, we were in fact operating as two equal naval forces with the necessary coordination, but with me as the undisputed commander of the Danish/Norwegian Task Group.

I did not recognise their assertion concerning overlapping coordination structures, as we had, as far as I was aware, established unequivocal coordination in time and space at the Moscow meeting. The OPCW and the UN set the time, meaning that they informed us of when to collect the chemical agents in Latakia. The space was where and how the ships should operate tactically during pickups, and the time in between pickups was, according to the Moscow Plan, to be coordinated between us and the coordination cell on board *Pyotr Velikiy*. The operation was thus fully coordinated, as we had two equal Task Group Commanders who, based on the Moscow Plan, would synchronise their individual plans to establish one joint plan. Surprisingly the Russians immediately accepted my line of reasoning, and we decided that as long as we kept each other informed, we would be able to complete any future pickups in Latakia according to the Moscow Plan. I think the real purpose of the Russian proposal was to test whether we would stick to the Moscow agreement. We stood firm, and that was the end of that.

At the meeting, we also discussed an exchange of liaison officers between *Esbern Snare* and *Pyotr Velikiy*. The commander of the cruiser announced that they, as a rule, did not see the necessity of having a liaison officer on board our ship, or the other way around, but they were ready to discuss this from time to time in connection with pickups.

One of Pyotr Velikiy's *dinghies returning the officers to the cruiser after the meeting on board* Esbern Snare *on 10 January. Unlike the Russians, the Chinese arrived in a helicopter from one of the frigates. When it landed on the Danish support ship, this represented the first time ever that a Chinese helicopter had landed on a Danish warship.*

Despite what I considered a – failed – Russian attempt to take control of the mission, the meeting ended well, and everyone was pleased that we now agreed on the tactical details supporting the Moscow Plan.

Following the meeting, I decided to scrub the idea of close cooperation with *Pyotr Velikiy* and the Chinese frigate, and I chose to send the following signal to the units in my Task Group:

Because of the unrest related to coordination between the two equal Task Groups of the maritime operation, this Task Group will not proactively engage with the Russian/Chinese Task Group. Until now we have offered training on an opportunity basis, but that has been cancelled until further notice. The Task Group will continue to answer their calls in a polite manner, and should they ask for specific matters which will force further interaction, you must find a way to end the conversation elegantly.

Furthermore, I want to stress that when activated for pickup of cargo in Latakia, it is of the outmost importance that we stick 100 per cent to the agreed quote Moscow unquote Plan. Make sure you write a good narrative and record communication, if possible.

The Task Group might expect a visit from Sigrid Kaag soon. Apparently, she wants to visit the seagoing parties. Due to the present unrest, I have suggested hosting the meeting on quote neutral ground unquote, e.g. on Cyprus.

Likewise, I sent the following to Frank Trojahn in Aarhus:

Will balance posture and act de-fuzing, as it is in everyone's interest to maintain a good relationship between the seagoing partners. Due to the present uncertainty, I will, on the other hand, ask the OPCW to be proactive and act as facilitator and buffer in case there is a need for that. Specifically, I see a role for the OPCW with regard to the planned coordination meeting for liaison activities on board Peter the Great on 20 Jan 2013. If the OPCW will be present at a sufficiently high level, I personally intend (unless otherwise directed) to attend.

Before we closed the meeting that day, the Russians called a new meeting on board *Pyotr Velikiy* on 20 January. The notice only applied to our liaison officer, however, but in light of developments during the that day's meeting, I decided to attend as well.

After a nice lunch in the officers' mess on *Esbern Snare*, the Russians and Chinese returned to their ships. Immediately afterwards I went to the bridge to participate – via video conference – in an event for relatives back home. The crew on *Esbern Snare* would soon be relieved by the crew that had worked on its sister ship, *Absalon*, back home. In that connection, the squadron in Denmark held an event at the naval base in Frederikshavn, where relatives could learn more about what their husbands, brothers, sisters, fathers or mothers would be doing in the Mediterranean. Via video conference I would be telling their relatives about the mission and the experiences and challenges their loved ones could expect to face during the three months of their deployment. But just before I was about to go on air, an unidentified smaller vessel was observed heading directly for *Taiko* at a speed of 30 knots. Our response was quick. As planned, *Helge Ingstad* remained put to protect *Ark Futura*, while *Esbern Snare* gained speed and headed towards the contact while issuing escalating warnings over the radio. After a couple of warnings, the vessel turned out to be a Turkish patrol boat that just wanted to see what was going on. Over the radio it was warned not to come too close, which the commander of the boat quickly realised was a good idea and changed its course. Subsequently, *Esbern Snare* could stand down and return to *Ark Futura*. The situation thus had a positive outcome, as it tested the ship's readiness and showed that everything worked according to our drills.

That night I had dinner in the cafeteria with the enlisted personnel. I usually took my meals in the officers' mess, but sometimes I like to make use of the sergeants' mess or the cafeteria. I did not do so too often, though, because I believe the NCOs and enlisted personnel should have a chance to discuss events on board without officers – in this case, me – listening in. However, the talk over dinner gave me some insight into what was happening among the enlisted personnel on board the support ship, and I left with the feeling that everyone was favourably disposed towards the mission.

After dinner, we had the usual evening meeting, where the staff gave me a detailed briefing of plans, weather, press, logistics, chemistry etc. for the upcoming days.

After the meeting, I ran into one of the frogmen who was exercising in the exercise room on the flex deck. I had a good relationship with these stout-hearted fellows and had known some of them since the 1990s, when I had served on one of the Navy's patrol vessels of the

Morning meeting in the officers' mess on Esbern Snare. *Life-saving coffee is being poured into the cups.*

Standard Flex class and participated in a series of operations and exercises alongside them. On several occasions during the current mission, they had invited me to join them on one of their daily trips to the sauna, where they seasoned the heat in the ship's sauna with camphor and peppermint to the brink of making you cry. That evening the frogman managed to persuade me to join them, and we had a really good chat in the heat, talking about shared memories from previous operations.

The next few days we continued the training. Thanks to the OPCW's GPS trackers – whose settings had now been adjusted – we were able to tell whether the containers were at the packing stations, along with the chemicals, or on their way to or from these stations. We could therefore be quite certain that we would have sufficient warning before the next pickup. The Russians and Chinese did not have immediate access to the GPS information, as their chain of command, as far as I knew, passed through Moscow and Beijing, respectively. This meant that they operated with a longer line of communication, whereas I could speak directly to our liaison officer, Commander Senior Grade Per Moll, at the OPCW mission headquarters in Cyprus.

The chief aim of the Task Group's extensive training was to make the five ships work together as one unit. This entailed doing a number of cross-ship exercises – at all hours. Considering the ships', on balance, limited staff resources, the training placed great demands on the staff to be persevering, but these exercises were necessary if we were to be ready for joint action. One night I learned that *Esbern Snare* on its own initiative had cancelled the night exercise. When I asked the sergeant on watch why the exercise had been cancelled, I was told that it was because we were less than 20 nautical miles from the coast of Syria. And the closer we were to the Syrian coast, the higher the level of readiness was required to due to the shorter warning time in the event of an attack. The exercise had therefore been cancelled to avoid working the crew unnecessarily hard. A sensible decision, as such, but I had to stress that I, as force commander, decided whether or not there was a need for training; it was not up to the individual ship commander. Whereas the commanders of the individual ships were responsible for their ship and crew, I was responsible for the entire naval force. This meant that I, together with my staff, scheduled the exercises that we believed were necessary, and if we found that training was necessary, the exercises were not an option. The decision to cancel exercises had to be approved by the staff based on a recommendation, and I was not completely satisfied with *Esbern Snare*'s decision to cancel the exercise that night. I strongly emphasised – not for the first time during the operation – to the staff officers and my staff operations and plans officer that they must try to rise above the individual ship level and view the situation holistically, namely that the fleet had to develop the ability to work together as closely as possible. We were not just responsible for *Esbern Snare*, whose crew, understandably, after months at sea might be less enthusiastic about the idea of more training. But even though the crew was tired and looked forward to going home soon, this was no popularity contest, and even if it was, the officers should be able to tolerate being unpopular if the aim was to increase the force members' ability to solve the task at hand. We were responsible for all four ships in the force, and if *Esbern Snare* cancelled an exercise, the state of readiness of the entire force suffered, not just ours.

Subsequently, the planned night exercise turned out to be realisable after all, even though we were close to Syrian territorial waters and the people in the CIC therefore had to work a bit harder to maintain a sufficient situational picture of the conditions surrounding the ship.

The following day was Sunday, and as usual when at sea we had a service on board. Naval ships on long-term missions far from home often bring a naval chaplain. In addition to his religious work, the naval chaplain also acts as pastoral carer to the crew, a role which has proved very valuable. On Sunday 12 January, the service took place in the cafeteria, and as always the chaplain (here called Father Frank) enjoyed great support from the crew, enough to make a normal Danish pastor envious. Almost everyone who was not on duty dropped by the cafeteria that had been beautifully adorned with a crucifix and candles.

That afternoon we practised sharp shooting in an area east of Cyprus. When we left the waters outside Latakia, *Pyotr Velikiy* remained just outside Syrian territorial waters until we were out of sight. Suddenly, the cruiser came rushing towards us at 30 knots, but once they could see us again, they stopped and lay still in the water. A strange approach, which I think was due to the fact that they simply did not have an up-to-date picture of what was happening at sea and in the air around them. They therefore did not have exact knowledge of the location of the individual units, aside from what was visible to the naked eye and a pair of binoculars.

Besides the large 127-milimetre cannon and sea- and air-target missiles, the support ships are also equipped with a number of machine guns for close combat. Here a member of the crew is practising with one of the light machine guns.

For shooting practice we used a so-called 'killer tomato' – an inflatable target placed a couple of thousand metres from the ship and usually capable of 'surviving' a number of hits before deflating and necessitating subsequent collection. Once all four units had completed the planned training, the 'killer tomato' was, despite several hits, still afloat. I then asked the officer on watch to call *Pyotr Velikiy* to offer them the target for practice. They might also wish to use the opportunity for a bit of practice shooting. However, they were not interested in using our target, they said they did their own training, using what they called a 'dinghy'. Everyone thought it was a bit strange on their part to turn down this opportunity, but it was not our decision to make.

I spent the rest of the afternoon responding to a question from the Danish Red-Green parliamentary alliance concerning the training of the civilian crew on board *Ark Futura*. Right from the start, I had been aware of the possibility of domestic political interference with the mis-

Pyotr Velikiy.

sion, and that politicians back home might begin to look for 'hairs in their soup' in order to present a negative view of an otherwise positive operation. I had seen it many times before in my various posts at Defence Command Denmark. Among other things, for several years I was involved on a daily basis in answering so-called Paragraph-20 questions of a more or less relevant nature. Of course, we had prepared for this, and the training of the civilian sailors had therefore been documented visually and in the form of course plans, so fortunately I did not have to spend all day answering questions.

The next couple of days *Esbern Snare* would be in Limassol, among other things to replace the majority of the crew members with the new crew fresh from Denmark. In that connection, we drew up a plan for what to do in case a pickup was announced while we were in Limassol. In that case, I and one of the staff officers would board *Helge Ingstad* and head the operation from there. The Norwegian Government had not granted *Esbern Snare* permission to protect *Taiko*, even though we had

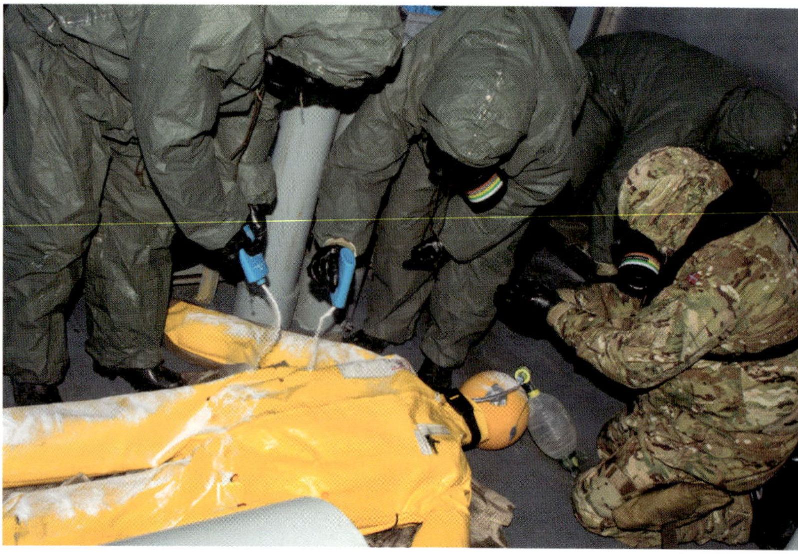

Exercise in handling a chemical accident on board Ark Futura.

granted *Helge Ingstad* permission to protect *Ark Futura*. This was another example of the differences between the Danish and Norwegian Rules of Engagement. These differences were, seen from my tactical level, unnecessarily limiting, but the decision had been made at a level above mine and was based on knowledge I did not have, and I therefore simply had to accept it and act accordingly.

That evening I had been invited to dine in the sergeants' mess, and just like my visit to the enlisted personnel's cafeteria a couple of days before it was an altogether enjoyable experience.

The next day, 14 January, began with the staff turnover on *Esbern Snare*. Among the crew members to return home were a couple of my staff officers, and I could therefore welcome a new military lawyer and a new liaison officer from the Danish Defence Intelligence Service, just as a new specialist in air operations, a so-called air liaison officer, joined us the following day. The latter was a sergeant from the Royal Danish Air Force, whom I had asked for specifically to help provide the necessary overview of the airspace surrounding the force.

On 14 January we also received a visit from the commander of the French frigate *Surcouf*. It was in the area on a French mission and thus not a part of our operation, but the commander was eager to meet to discuss the opportunity to train with us. A suggestion toward which we were favourably disposed.

That morning I also had a meeting with our liaison officer at the OPCW mission headquarters in Cyprus, Per Moll. Per had vented his frustrations about the fact that the OPCW personnel changed every two weeks. Roughly speaking, this meant that he had to start over again each time, answering the same questions over and over. I could understand his frustration with the lack of focus on continuity in an organisation which – in their own words – was put in place to facilitate the completion of the mission. True or not, unfortunately it left us with the impression that the UN and OPCW did not have sufficient interest in the operation.

Furthermore, the OPCW had announced that they expected Operation RECSYR to be completed by the summer of 2014. This meant that they did not plan for the eventuality that the pickups might be further delayed. In light of the fact that the operation had already been delayed considerably, and that we had so far only completed one pickup, we felt that the OPCW was being unrealistically optimistic. As part of the Danish Defence we were used to drawing up 'what if' plans, but it was our impression that such an approach was not in vogue in the more political organisations.

After my meeting with Per Moll, one of the frogmen called me. He thought I needed some air and invited me to join him on a boat to *Ark Futura*, which was outside Limassol, approximately 15 nautical miles from the port. Due to its cargo of chemical agents, the ship was not allowed to dock in Limassol or even to enter Cypriot territorial waters. A bit of a paradox: The whole world wanted to see the chemical agents leave Syria, but no one would allow the agents to enter their territorial waters or ports.

I naturally accepted the offer, put on my raincoat and life jacket and off we went. At the dinghy's top speed of approx. 50 knots, it did not take us long to reach *Ark Futura*, and the ride was fun, to put it mildly.

The frogmen had to collect something on board *Ark Futura*, and I chose to join them as I wanted to say hello to the commander. He did not know I was coming and was very surprised to see me in the mess. He and part of the crew were returning home the next day, so I was happy to be able to say goodbye for now. Commander Niels invited me to join

Containers on the deck of Ark Futura.

them for a meal of meatballs in curry sauce, and afterwards we went down to inspect the cargo. Niels stressed that the containers had been carefully secured and that it would take a lot for them to topple over. This was very reassuring to hear.

On 15 January the British frigate *Montrose* joined the force. It arrived in Limassol at 09:00, and as planned Commander James Parkin joined me on *Esbern Snare* shortly afterwards for a meeting followed by lunch. The kind and punctual British naval officer made a good first impression, and we had a good chat about the operation.

15 January was also the day of the planned staff turnover on *Esbern Snare*. At 14:00 the around 120 members of staff returning home would leave on busses for the airport, and I was at the jetty from 13:15 and until they had left to shake the hands of as many of them as possible. It was important for me to be there to thank them. They had all worked hard to prepare and had done a really good job, and I wanted them to know that I had noticed and appreciated this.

This kind of farewell is always a bit sad, and the atmosphere among those of us who were staying was a bit sullen at first – especially among those who, regardless of what had now been a long-term deployment, would not return home yet for various reasons. Once the busses had departed, there were very few of us left on *Esbern Snare*. It was a ghostly experience to walk around the empty ship that was suddenly silent after having hummed with activity.

Three hours later, at 17:00, the new crew arrived. I returned to the jetty to welcome each new crew member. It was easy, because they had to walk up the gangway, and there I was, ready to shake their hand. I do not think they expected me to, to be honest, and a lot of them looked very surprised to see me, as the first person to welcome them, but I felt it was the right signal to send.

Subsequently, the situation on board was a bit chaotic, as was to be expected, because the ship had to be prepared for all the new faces who had to unpack. Even so, the bustle was over rather soon, as everyone knew the ship and their place on board.

Our Relationship with the Russians Deteriorates

During the first weeks of January 2014, it became clear that our relationship with the Russians was changing, and not for the better, I am afraid. We had seen the first signs of a change at the meeting on 10 January, where I had managed to foil the Russian attempt to take control of the operation. I thought the case had been settled there, but late in the evening on 15 January I learned that the Russians had filed a formal complaint with the OPCW concerning the pickup on 7 January.

The Russians claimed that we had failed to contact them that day before entering Syrian territorial waters. They felt that this did not live up to the Moscow Agreement's notion of 'partner-like' behaviour. In addition, they claimed that Denmark was trying to 'coup' itself into being the leading nation and that my force, unlike the Russians, was not ready to respond at all hours.

The Russians therefore repeated their wish to create a coordination cell on board *Pyotr Velikiy* permanently staffed with liaison officers from all the participating countries, but under Russian control. Of course we could not agree to this – in fact, I considered the formation of such a coordination cell a coup of the very kind the Russians were accusing us of perpetrating!

This constituted a clear violation of the agreement we had signed in Moscow on 27 December 2013, and in my answer to the Chief of the Naval Staff, I was able to refute all allegations that we had failed to keep the Russians informed. The Russian approach vexed me, but at the same time it was clear to all of us that neither I nor the Danish ships were the crux of the matter. We had simply become pawns in a political game between great powers. After having been forced to its knees in the 1990s and the first part of the '00s, Russia had now managed to get back on its feet financially, and this resulted in the country's increased presence on the international scene. Russia wanted to come across as a modern country, able to join humanitarian operations, just as they had secured the hosting of the 2014 Winter Olympics in Sochi and played an active part in the peace talks in Geneva, which in the spring of 2014 attempted to bring an end to the Syrian civil war. And now they were trying to take control of Operation RECSYR.

As part of the complaint, the Russians announced that due to their dissatisfaction with the situation they refused to participate in the press coordination group set up by the OPCW in Cyprus – even though the group had been established by request from the Russians and Syrians who, as mentioned, had demanded that reporters not be allowed on board the ships.

The press coordination group had already been formed, and headed by the Danish ambassador in Cyprus, Casper Klynge, it would have comprised representatives from Great Britain, the US, Russia, China and the OPCW. But now the Russians did not want to contribute to the group after all.

While the political game played out at the strategic level, we continued at the tactical level to prepare for the next pickup. As soon as *Esbern Snare*'s new crew had settled in, we left the port. While *Helge Ingstad* docked in Limassol, we took over responsibility for protecting *Ark Futura* and *Taiko*, which were still in the holding area between Cyprus and Syria, waiting for the next shipment of chemical agents. I spent the day thinking about how I should address the cooperation with the Russians in light of their announcements the previous day. Both the OPCW and Danish authorities back home had given me their full support, and we were able to document in writing and communication recordings that we had acted completely as agreed in Moscow. This did not change the fact that the situation was somewhat stuck. We ended up asking UN diplomat Sigrid Kaag to contact the Russian deputy foreign minister to try to explain what had happened and determine whether the Moscow Plan had to be adjusted.

The next couple of days were relatively quiet. The new crews on board *Esbern Snare* and *Ark Futura* had to find their feet in the mission, which did not take long, though, as both crews came well-prepared.

On 17 January I was able to visit Montrose. Together with my Norwegian deputy commander, I was given a three-hour tour of the ship and what they had done to prepare for the mission. The crew came across as professional through and through. At the time, they had not been home for six months, but they were ready for what might come. Seeing their motivation to support me and the mission was a very positive experience, and I gained a very good impression of the commander of the ship who appeared to have a very good handle on his crew.

We agreed to do a joint Force Protection exercise for Montrose and *Esbern Snare* the following Sunday, 19 January. As the crew on *Esbern Snare* was new, both ships needed to practise response in the event of an attack from smaller, fast-moving vessels, which is a well-known and commonly used method for attacking cargo ships.

Once I had returned to *Esbern Snare* I had our military linguist call the Russians to say that our Deputy Commander, our liaison officer and I would participate in the meeting on 20 January. After making the call, the military linguist returned to tell me that the Russian reply had somewhat surprisingly been that I and the Deputy Commander should not participate. Furthermore, they had said that the intention was not to hold a meeting, but to invite our liaison officer to join them on Monday and to remain on board the Russian cruiser throughout the rest of Operation RECSYR.

David, my military linguist specialised in Russian, who had participated in the December meeting in Moscow, had informed the Russians that this was not in agreement with the Moscow Plan, and that we therefore could not agree to it. In response the Russians had said they would get back to us once they had discussed the situation on board. They could discuss as much as they wanted to, but we were not about to change our minds. I did not want to have a permanent liaison officer on board *Pyotr Velikiy*.

This development worried me. It was clear that the Russians had discovered the political advantage of coming across as being the ones who called the shots, and they were still very determined to take control of Operation RECSYR.

I enjoyed spending time with the 'new' crew. I had demanded a lot of them during exercises the past year. In fact, as commander of the Second Squadron I had 'failed' the ship during an exercise in 2013 because it had not been ready for combat. This rarely happens, and it is not amusing for the commander of a ship to be barred from a planned exercise and instead having to remain in port until having addressed deficiencies. Now, however, they were 100 per cent ready for the job. (MoD)

Later that night I received a message from our liaison officer at the OPCW mission headquarters in Cyprus, Per Moll. He announced that he had been contacted by the American liaison officer there because the commander of the US fleet, Admiral Jonathan Greenert, had asked him who was Officer in Tactical Command (commander of the joint fleet) of the maritime operation in the eastern Mediterranean. We agreed that the cause of the US enquiry was another Russian attempt to take control of the operation. After we had refused to submit to the Russians by transferring our liaison officers to the Russian ship, they may have tried to convince the Americans that the command and coordination of the operation was uncertain. Together, Per Moll and I produced an answer to the Americans, where I made it clear that there was no commander of the joint fleet. There were two independent commanders with two independent Task Groups, who coordinated their efforts in connection with the pickups in Syria, but this was carried out as discussions between authorities of the same rank. I also forwarded my operation concept to the Americans and made it clear that this operational concept was based on the Moscow Plan from December 2013 upon which all the parties had agreed.

Naturally, I immediately informed Frank Trojahn in Aarhus of events and what I believed had prompted them. I recommended him to have someone back home – if they had not done so already – establish contact with the countries responsible for the operation in order to discuss how we should act in case events made it impossible for us to continue to follow the Moscow Plan.

In the middle of this process, I suddenly received another email from Per Moll, who could inform me that the commander of the Russian fleet had contacted Damascus to tell them that *Ark Futura* lacked fuel and to ensure that fuel would be waiting for the ship next time it docked in Latakia. The problem was that after having received the cargo of chemical agents, only two ports were open to *Ark Futura*: Latakia and the British port where we expected to unship the chemical agents after completing the operation. So, unlike *Esbern Snare*, for example, the cargo ship could not dock in Limassol for fresh supplies, and it did not have the same equipment as the warships that would have enabled it to refuel on the open sea.

The Russian request could only be interpreted as another attempt to appear as the actual commander of the operation. As I would not acknowledge the Russians' right to interfere with my dispositions concerning the *Ark Futura*'s fuel supply – or anything else, for that matter – I asked our military linguist to call the Russians to deliver a formal and clear message:

For CTG RF Commander Peshkurov from CTG 420.01, Flotilla Admiral Mikkelsen.

Dear colleague,

I have learned that you have expressed concern regarding fuel and refuelling of Ark Futura. *I thank you for your concern, but I will handle the matter via the agreements made under the auspices of the OPCW. For your information, the ship's agent and the agent appointed by Syria will handle the matter.*

Kind regards,
Flotilla Admiral Torben Mikkelsen, CTG 420.01

Russian 'spy ship' off the coast of Syria.

The Russian reply was that they could have offered to help, and I ended up thanking him for their concern, but that their help was not required.

At the same time, I brought up the issue of transferring a liaison officer to *Pyotr Velikiy*. Once again, the Russians passed it off as a misunderstanding. We then said goodnight, and that was the end of the conversation.

Concurrently with their attempt to take political control of Operation RECSYR, the Russians increased their number of warships in the area off the coast of Syria. We had for some time been followed by a Russian 'spy ship', whose multitude of antennas were able to intercept everything we talked about on the radio, the phone and in emails. It was like having been transported back in time to the Cold War. Russian helicopters would even fly over us from time to time to take pictures of everything we did.

The presence of the Russian units did not make us change plans, however. On 20 January we conducted a series of shooting exercises in an area east of Cyprus assigned for such exercises. Shooting exercises are always

Maintenance of Esbern Snare's *front-most 35-mm CIWS.*

good for morale and the mood on board. Unfortunately, we had suffered a breakdown in the front-most CIWS (Close-In Weapon System). It had broken down and we had sent for spare parts, which would arrive from Denmark in a couple of days. *Esbern Snare* was equipped with two CIWS systems, whose very high rate of fire protected the ship from missiles and the like. The fact that 50 per cent of our close defence was down was not catastrophic, though; by turning the ship around, the CIWS astern could engage with potential enemy targets. Nevertheless, we were most comfortable with having access to both systems when operating close to the coast of Syria.

After completing the shooting exercise, the fleet moved to the holding area outside Latakia where we would, according to the Moscow Plan, wait for the next shipment of chemical agents. I moved the ships from the area outside Limassol to the holding area because this would enable us to pick up the next shipment with short notice, but also because I was tired of having to defend my dispositions to the Russians. We would now follow the Moscow Plan as closely as possible and communicate to the world that we were ready – and had been so for a long time.

Deckhand at one of Esbern Snare's 12.7-millimetre machine guns. Ark Futura *is in the background.*

At the strategic level the political game and semantic exercises continued. That afternoon I received a report from the Danish Ambassador in Cyprus, Casper Klynge, informing us that the Russians had increased pressure on the OPCW. During a meeting between Sigrid Kaag and the Russian Ambassador to Cyprus, Stanislav V. Osadchiy, the latter had, irreconcilably, repeated the Russian complaint concerning my dispositions on 7 January. The Russians accused me directly of not having lived up to the Moscow Agreement, claiming that the Agreement stated that Russia would be responsible of the overall coordination of the operation. I therefore did not have a mandate, according to the Russians, to act as I had in connection with the pickup, and they thus considered my dispositions unacceptable.

The Russians were also resentful of the fact that their participation in the 7 January pickup had not been mentioned in the OPCW press statements on the matter. The Russian Ambassador accused the OPCW of having allowed Denmark and Norway to change the wording of the press release, removing all reference to the Russian and Chinese participation and thus taking full credit for the successful operation.

On 20 January Esbern Snare *received a visit from the Finnish general responsible for the seven chemical specialists from the Finnish Army on board the ship. The general's visit was a clear sign of the significance Finland attached to its participation in the operation. I had therefore decided to use the helicopter on* Esbern Snare *to pick up the Finnish delegation, giving them a chance to get an overview of the fleet from the air – both those who were part of our force and the Russian and Chinese ships. During the visit, we conducted an exercise simulating a chemical spill on board* Ark Futura, *where the Finnish specialists would act as the Quick Reaction Force. The exercise was a success, and we managed to convey to Finland that their contribution was important and very useful. In the photo, preparations are being made to hoist a gas-affected extra into the helicopter during the exercise on 20 January.*

At the meeting, Sigrid Kaag had repudiated the Russian allegations. Nowhere did the Moscow Agreement dictate that Russia would be responsible for the overall coordination of the operation, just as it was incorrect of the Russians to claim that Denmark or others had adjusted the OPCW press statements. They had been produced at the OPCW mission headquarters in Cyprus, and the Russian and Chinese ships were not mentioned in connection with the first pickup because they had only played a minor role in the operation.

In conclusion Sigrid Kaag had asked for a telephone meeting with the Russian Deputy Foreign Minister on the case, giving her a chance to resolve the conflict at a higher level.

I spent much time the next few days thinking about how we at our level could try to resolve the intensifying conflict with the Russians. The OPCW had informed me that the Syrians were likely to have another shipment of chemical agents ready for pickup in Latakia within the next six to eight days. Just like last time I was almost certain that this information would not reach the Russians on board *Pyotr Velikiy*, unless I did not do something to make sure it did. If I called the Russian force commander to tell him, it would, on the one hand, demonstrate that I intended to live up to our agreement of keeping each other informed, but on the other hand, it could prove problematic in relation to Moscow, because I was certain that he did not receive this kind of information, and if I chose to inform him, he would undoubtedly inform Moscow, who might find that I was acting as the supreme coordinator and commander of the operation. I decided to sleep on it first.

Inspired by the Russians' behaviour, we conducted an exercise on 22 January simulating a situation where the Russians on board *Pyotr Velikiy* tried to take control of the mission. My staff played the role of the Russians and were tasked with trying to take control. The tools available to them in such a situation were of course wholly diplomatic and communicative, and the aim of the exercise was to ensure that everyone involved had full knowledge of the Moscow Plan, and that any Russian attempt to take control would be met with friendly insistence that we were acting in accordance with the agreed plan and by agreement with the OPCW mission headquarters in Cyprus. Such insistence on our part would demonstrate that we were not working for Russia, but that we ranked alongside them and were partners with the Russians and only subjected to the OPCW and the UN.

The exercise was a success and an instructive experience for everyone. At the same time, I had reached a decision on whether or not to inform the Russian force commander of the coming pickup. I did not expect him to inform me in a similar situation, but that should not keep me from doing it. In all other cases, I would make sure to keep my colleagues informed, and that is also what I chose to do here. I therefore asked my military linguist to deliver the following message to *Pyotr Velikiy*:

The Russian Ropucha-class landing ships – here the Kaliningrad *photographed in the Baltic Sea during an exercise in 2012 – can carry up to 480 tons each.*

Dear colleague,

I have learned that containers are likely to be ready for pickup in Latakia within the next 6-8 days. As we agreed to share information with each other on 10 January, I hereby share this knowledge with you.

Kind regards,
Flotilla Admiral Torben Mikkelsen

According to the military linguist who spoke to the Russian force commander in person, he sounded surprised but also happy to have been informed.

During the night of 22 and 23 January, another two Russian warships arrived in the area: two large landing ships of the Ropucha class. My first thought was whether they could be used to pick up the second-priority agents whose handling we in the West still did not have a plan for. The job of destroying the chemical agents had been put out to commercial tender, but so far no country had volunteered. The Russians had announced publicly that they were capable of destroying the second-priority agents safely. I therefore feared that the Syrians would suddenly announce that the next shipment would contain both first- and second-priority agents. If they did so before we had found someone to receive the second-priority agents, the Russians might use this as a pretext to include their ships as active players in the operation. At this point in

We spent the afternoon of 23 January conducting an exercise with the French frigate Surcouf, *here at the top of the photo, alongside the American destroyer* Stout. *The commander of* Surcouf *turned out to be friends with a French officer whom I had taken a course with in the US. With our mutual friend acting as a form of liaison officer, we managed to get a couple of successful exercises going. (A.R. Gray/U.S. Navy)*

time, our plan was to carry the second-priority agents to Norway, on board *Taiko*, but everyone doubted that we would be able to gain political backing before picking up the next shipment in Latakia. All I could do at my level was to ask my intelligence staff to draw up a report on the issue. It was forwarded to the Naval Command and Defence Command Denmark in the hope that the report would help speed up the decision-making process.

At the same time, we made a plan for how to act in case *Ark Futura* and *Taiko* had to enter the port of Latakia simultaneously. Such an event was not described in the Moscow Plan, but we found a way to handle it 'in the spirit' of the plan to avoid more accusations of not living up to the agreement.

On the evening of 23 January, I learned that the Danish Minister for Foreign Affairs would be visiting us the following Sunday. This came as a surprise, as three days' notice was not much for a ministerial visit, and this immediately before a probable pickup in Latakia. The decision, which unfortunately had been made without involving me or anyone from my staff, was not sensible tactically, and could give our Chinese and Russian colleagues the impression that we did not take our job seriously.

Before entering Latakia, we should be allowed time to gain an overview of events (a so-called Pattern of Life) in the area to determine whether everything was as it should be. To do so we had to be present in the area outside of Latakia, not off the coast of Cyprus with a minister on board. I therefore informed the Naval Command back home that it would be unwise tactically if the minister's visit were to coincide with a pickup. We needed about 24 hours in the area off Syria before a pickup, just as we had to have time to move from Cyprus to the area, and this simply did not allow time for such a visit. This information was passed on to Defence Command Denmark and the Danish Ministry of Defence, and I was pleased to receive a message the next day saying that the minister's visit had been postponed to a more suitable date. Sometimes it is simply hard to see why such a request has to reach the operational theatre before someone reacts.

24 January

We have received a new crew, and they should also be allowed a chance to try to tow *Ark Futura*. Unlike last time, though, one of *Esbern Snare*'s main motors has had a defect for the past 4-5 days, and naturally that limits our ability to manoeuvre. A bolt in the cylinder head is defective, a rather big bolt, mind you. It is one metre long and 50 mm in diameter. Very different from your standard bolt. Well, a new one is on its way on board *Montrose*, which leaves in the morning. Then both engines can get up and running again.

We may – as a worst-case scenario – have to be able to tow *Ark Futura* out of Syrian waters fast. I have therefore asked the crew to practise this and make sure it is feasible. The towing went well. If *Ark Futura* should suffer engine problems, we will be able to assist before the actual tugboats arrive.

We can tell that a couple of American Arleigh Burke-class destroyers (USS *Stout* and USS *Ramage*) are on their way to the area from the south. At one point we received a message from USS *Stout* saying that they intend to drop by. I replied: 'Welcome. Good to see you'. When considering the large number of Russian units in the area, I am certain that they will know what I mean.

Towing exercise with Ark Futura.

The commanders, executive officers and I have been invited to lunch on board *Surcouf*, so the French helicopter came to pick all of us up and dropped us on the French unit. Thomas, the commander, is a really nice fellow, and they treated us to a delicious meal and a tour of the ship. It was fun to see the frigate, which is almost 20 years old now. I remember when it was the latest new thing, back when I saw one of its sister ships in a James Bond film. How time flies.

On 24 January we received a message saying that 26 January would almost certainly be the day of the next pickup in Latakia. This piece of information also reached Defence Command Denmark back home, where the officer on watch chose to share this information with the rest of the world in a briefing sent from the command's official email. This somewhat slipshod behaviour directly compromised our safety, and it made me so furious that I immediately sent them an angry email. Syrian rebel forces might use this knowledge to prepare an attack, now that they knew when we would call into port in Latakia. I received an apology from home within minutes, where they promised to mend their ways. This episode is another example of the different perspectives of the staff back home and units deployed on a mission. There is a natural dilemma between sharing information with the people we work for back home and our need for discretion for security reasons.

In connection with the pickup on 26 January, I decided to call into port with *Ark Futura*. During the first pickup, I had commanded the operation from *Esbern Snare*, but I had been told that the Syrian colonel responsible for security in Latakia was the same colonel I had met in Moscow in December 2013. He had proven as being easy to talk to, and I felt that my presence at the jetty would send a positive signal.

At the same time, it would also be a good signal to send the crew on *Ark Futura* and our contribution in container scanner for me to be present in Latakia. I therefore asked the commander of the frogmen to assess the safety conditions in Latakia and determine whether it was advisable for me to join them.

At the same time, I decided that as soon as we received official notice from the OPCW concerning the pickup, I would call my Russian colleague and inform him.

25 January

You can almost sense a kind of Saturday quiet on board the ship. All the ships are now lying side by side in the holding area by the call of the port, waiting, and we are all looking at each other, a somewhat unique sensation. Here we are, 6-7 ships, approx. 2,000 men, plus the ones on board the other ships in the area, which are not directly affiliated with the pickup. I guess about 5,000 to 7,000 people are currently working on this – and that is just out here. Add to this all the people of the UN and the OPCW, not to mention Russia and Syria on land. It is a bit crazy.

I do not know why we still have not received official notification of our call to port tomorrow morning. We have been told that we will be given 24 hours' notice, so I am a bit worried about what is happening. I called our liaison officer in Cyprus, who got in touch with Latakia. The report is still that OPCW/UN staff and Syrians are pouring into Latakia. That has to be a good sign. But we still lack the official notification, and I cannot coordinate the operation with my Russian colleague before this is official.

During the day, it became clear to me that the pickup would probably be postponed until Monday. And we have received a communication this afternoon from Cyprus. The good thing is that the shipment we are to collect in Latakia will probably be larger than expected.

Suddenly, I receive a second call from Per Moll telling me that he had spoken to the Danish Ministry of Defence, who have argued that Norway can easily accept loading the second-priority shipments!

Overall, this is extremely positive, of course, because now we finally have the flexibility we need. But still, it is amazing that we have to come all this way and get this close before something happens. You almost get the feeling that we have to fear that the Russians will steal it from right under our noses before someone reacts.

Well, easy now! But sometimes it can be difficult to control your temper. After all, I am the one who has to make this work with a large naval concentration and the danger of criticism from Moscow and subsequent strategic consequences even if I do everything completely by the book.

At around 17:00, we then received an official announcement from Norway, saying that they are ready to receive whatever shipments might come. This is perfect and very courageous of Norway, seeing as we were still waiting for someone to volunteer to receive the second-priority agents.

I have received a reply concerning my request to enter Latakia on board *Ark Futura*. The assessment is that I in that case should be treated as a VIP and thus receive protection in the form of bodyguards from among the frogmen. They are not happy about the idea of me going ashore. Out of respect for the Syrian officers in the port, including General Sharif, my plan was to go ashore once the ramp was out and introduce myself to my friend from Moscow, the colonel, who would probably be waiting at the jetty. At least he was there last time. I want to show them the respect of going ashore without protective gear, just like the Syrians. I just want to say hello, thank them for cooperating, do a bit of small talk and then return to *Ark Futura*.

However, the frogmen have assessed that I would constitute an inviting target to the rebel forces, and I would therefore require protection in the form of bodyguards and protective gear. I will not go ashore. I do not want them to expend resources on me. These are better spent protecting what it's all about: the personnel going ashore in Latakia, the shipment and *Ark Futura*.

Later this evening, I received an official communication from Latakia, with a description of the shipment saying that we will be calling into port on the 27th. And then, we are disappointed again: It's a small shipment!

We spent 26 January preparing for the pickup. When we had been told that the next shipment would be larger than the first, I had decided that both *Taiko* and *Ark Futura* would call into port this time. I hoped that this would also give *Ark Futura* a chance to refuel.

However, late that night we were told that the shipment was a lot smaller than we had first anticipated and this made me consider postponing the operation altogether for security reasons. I had to weigh the amount of chemical agents in the shipment against the security risk of calling into port several times. Because each time we called into port in Latakia, the rebel forces could observe how we operated; and if we did this too many times, they might be able to predict our dispositions, which would increase their chances of conducting a successful attack against us. After having thought about it, I nevertheless decided to go through with the pickup – for strategic reasons, not giving the Russians and Syrians further grounds for which to criticise me.

A Syrian pilot boat being monitored closely by the Frogman Corps.

The Second Pickup

27 January
All the ships were waiting in the holding area, and our communication with the Russians went well. As agreed in Moscow, a liaison officer was transferred, but we were suddenly told that the Russians also wanted to transfer two of their liaison officers to *Esbern Snare*. All right, but they have to stay on the bridge. We do not want them running around inside the ship.

We were at general quarters with everyone in place wearing the right gear, including fire-resistant face masks and gloves as well as helmets, flak jackets and glasses for those on the bridge and on deck. As we approached Latakia, we could tell that there was a lot of security in the port. The harbour and piers were soon declared 'clear' and the ships were ready to enter the port.

Force commander on the open bridge while putting into port at Latakia.

It soon turned out not to be possible to refuel *Ark Futura* in Latakia, as the Syrians were unable to tell us which type of fuel they could provide. This is a challenge, because *Ark Futura* must refuel at some point, and as things stand, the ship can only dock in two countries in the world, Syria and Great Britain, the country receiving the shipment it is carrying.

Suddenly the port announced that they were displeased with the fact that people on board the Norwegian cargo ship were taking photos and making video recordings. Dammit. We have spoken about this in detail, and everyone knows that it is important to the Norwegians to be able to profile the operation in the press. It is really unsatisfactory that we now risk running afoul of the Syrians – the situation with Russia at the strategic level is difficult enough, and I do not need any more challenges right now.

We are then informed that some of the containers must be repackaged before they can be loaded. The reason for this is that they have come from sites where the OPCW has been unable to monitor the packing, and they therefore have to be checked before they can be approved. Of course, this is the safest choice, but they should really have done this before we docked. After all, they knew they had to be repackaged! Now, here we are with several ships and a lot of people in a not too secure area. They must be able to do better next time.

At the same time – in the midst of things – we had to consider a press release. I had to go down to my cabin to read it. It was a generic statement from the OPCW on the pickup of chemical agents in Syria, and it could have been written and sent out for consultation two weeks ago, but of course it had to be done right now in the Syrian port!

Well, I am happy that I got a chance to read it, because the OPCW had 'forgotten' to include Great Britain and Finland in the list of participating nations. After several emails back and forth, and a couple of hours later, the OPCW admitted that they did not wish to mention Great Britain as they did not think the Syrians knew that a British warship was participating in the operation. I then had to tell them that this was not the case. I had mentioned this explicitly in Moscow, where everyone – including the Syrians – had been present, just as I had mentioned this point at the two meetings with the Russians and Chinese.

I know why they do not wish to mention Great Britain. It is because the British, together with the US, were prepared to go to war with Syria last August. Therefore, it does not 'suit' the OPCW to mention them – what if it made the Syrians angry? That is their problem. I have told them that the Syrians already know. Whether they choose to leave them out deliberately, I will leave unstated. But I do not think it is right to indulge al-Assad this way and not to consider the importance of mentioning all the contributing nations.

Due to the repackaging, the pickup took all day, and we had to suffer the heat in our protective gear – helmet, hat, gloves and bulletproof jacket are just not the right fit for a seaman. Everything went well, though, and that evening I could send the following signal to the ships in my force:

A long, but good day at sea. Seen from a Task Group planning and execution point of view, today's operation went smoothly. Both internally in our own Task Group and also between the two Task Groups. A two-ship run-in with Helge Ingstad *and* Esbern Snare *as close escorts and* Montrose *as back stopper has now been tested and it worked as planned. Additionally, the liaison plan was tested, and according to feedback from the Danish liaison officer upon his return from* Pyotr Velikiy, *it went smoothly and was necessary to ensure a smooth cooperation. Two Russian liaison officers embarked* Esbern Snare *today, and we must prepare to host Russian liaison officer(s) during future pickups. A thing worth mentioning while waiting for your After Action Reports and Lessons Identified is the security issue related to waiting for containers to be ready for embarkation. This must be improved in the future, and I intend to put forward that containers have to be ready for embarkation when we enter Latakia.*

Additionally, the limited number of containers today is also an issue that has to be considered and not least balanced against the risk of entering Latakia. In future run-ins I will request more containers. Security issues are not only a concern for OPCW personnel in Latakia, but a general concern. Your After Action Reports and Lessons Identified will be used for Task Group feedback to the OPCW.

All in all, a successful and rewarding day with good Task Group cooperation and a high degree of professionalism.

Again, thank you all for a job well done.

At the same time, an almost identical signal was sent to Frank Trojahn back home in Aarhus.

On 28 January *Esbern Snare* conducted a so-called Replenishment at Sea (RAS) operation off the coast of Syria. The support ship's two engines used a lot of fuel, and we could not really do without the ship for the time it would take to dock in Limassol for refuelling. We therefore arranged for a meeting with a US supply ship which transferred approx. 150,000 litres of diesel to *Esbern Snare* on the open sea. The RAS completed, we turned around and headed toward *Montrose*, which had been protecting *Taiko* and *Ark Futura* that night, as both ships were now carrying containers.

Just before noon, the doctor on *Ark Futura* informed us that one of the seamen on board had developed symptoms of a blood clot. After some

Replenishment at Sea. I had to get up and out on deck to see the virtues of the time-honoured naval techniques for myself. Manoeuvring two ships of this size sailing at 10-15 knots, only 30-40 metres apart, requires ingenuity and experience. There is something fascinating about such maritime skill, which includes a burdensome but nevertheless precise effort on deck, working hawsers, wires and hoses as well as manoeuvring efforts to keep the two moving ships close to each other. Here the fuelling hose is approaching Esbern Snare. *(K.E. Huus)*

deliberation on the matter, the doctor on *Ark Futura* and the one on board *Esbern Snare* decided that the seaman in question had to be taken to a hospital in Cyprus. *Ark Futura* was located a good distance from us and far from the coast, but the support ship's helicopter could manage the trip out to the ship and into Cyprus.

You usually have to give 48 hours' notice before being allowed to enter another country's airspace, but in emergencies you naturally do not have to wait for permission. The problem then is being allowed to exit, and you risk having to wait 48 hours on ground before receiving permission to take off. We thus risked having to make do without the helicopter for two days. A clever chap then suggested calling the Danish Ambassador in Cyprus, and in a matter of minutes he had procured the necessary permission for Blue Ghost to land in Cyprus with the ill seaman. Having solved the problem, it turned out that the seaman in question did not want to be flown to a Cypriot hospital after all. We chose to ignore him, though. If the ship's doctor felt that he had to go to a hospital, then he *had* to go to a hospital. We could not have persons on board who required special attention, or who were unfit to do their job. They might put the mission and their shipmates at risk, and we could not accept such a risk. After all, next time he felt poorly might be in the middle of a pickup in Syria. Consequently, he and *Esbern Snare*'s helicopter went off to Limassol. The medical examination showed that he was fine, and after a couple of days in a hotel in Limassol he returned to *Ark Futura* on board *Helge Ingstad*, which had been in Limassol on other business.

In late January, we could sense a new challenge looming on the horizon. At this point we had only collected around five per cent of the expected amount of chemical agents, so we still had a long way to go. We therefore had to plan for the eventuality that the operation might continue well into 2014. Such a delay would entail that the Second Squadron would 'run out of' crew for *Esbern Snare*. The Danish Navy had at its disposal two crews for the two support ships, and as a rule, we operated with a rotation system which meant that the crew under normal circumstances were deployed for three months at a time and then went home on leave for three months. *Esbern Snare* had already been deployed for most of 2013 and would, beginning in May 2014 and throughout the rest of the year, serve as flagship in the Standing NATO Maritime Group 1 with the Commander of the Royal Danish Navy's Tactical Staff as force commander. If Operation RECSYR were to drag on, we

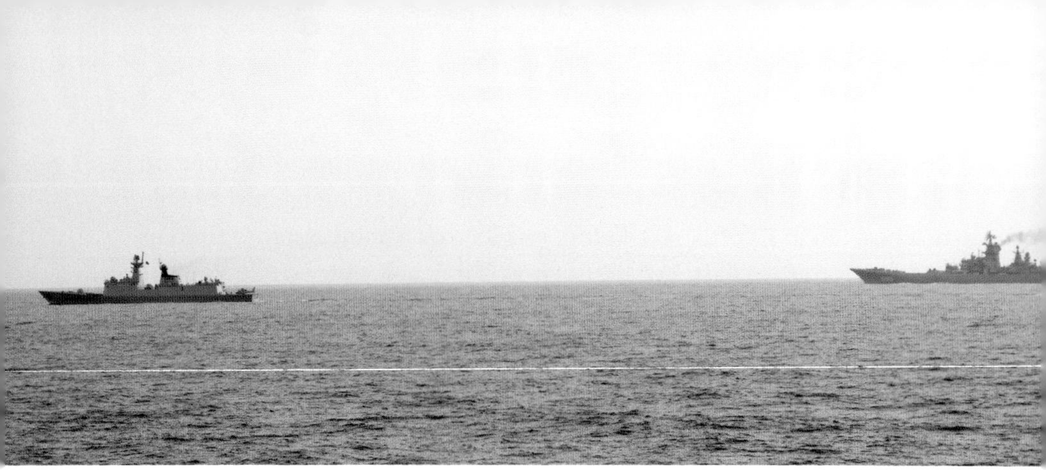

On the evening of 31 January, I called the Chinese frigate on the radio to wish them a Happy New Year, as China entered the Year of the Horse that night. They were happy to hear from me. As we sailed towards them to get within radio range, we could see that the entire frigate had been festooned with celebratory lights, and they were setting off fireworks. It looked really festive! The photo shows Yancheng *under more normal circumstances, here together with* Pyotr Velikiy *on the right.*

would therefore have to replace *Esbern Snare* with either *Absalon* or one of the Navy's three frigates of the Iver Huitfeldt class. However, the *Absalon* crew could not be deployed without breaking the rotation principle, and this meant that we either had to put together a crew for *Absalon* from one of the three frigates or send one of the three frigates at the beginning of May. In order to prepare for this scenario, we therefore began to plan for what to do in case *Absalon* or the frigate *Peter Willemoes* had to replace *Esbern Snare* in the mission area.

January ended with a call into port in Limassol. We had to take on fresh supplies, just as the crew had to have a chance to go ashore to experience the town and the local culture. When I returned to the ship that evening after dinner at a local restaurant, I dropped by the officer on watch for a status report on the units still at sea. Everything was in order, but to my great surprise a signal from Per Moll was waiting for me. He informed me that the Syrian general, Sharif, who was responsible for the transportation of the containers in Syria had filed several written complaints after the pickup in Latakia last Monday. One of his lorries had broken down, and several others required maintenance, and to solve this problem the general asked us to transfer a million US dollars. Naturally, no such amount would ever be transferred to the general, but the mere fact that he tried to profit from the situation said a lot about his approach to the entire operation and his work as an officer, from my point of view.

Esbern Snare's *commander, Søren Thinggaard Larsen, giving the Cypriot Minister of Foreign Affairs, Ioannis Kasoulides, a tour of the support ship.*

Not because of the general's request, but because of bad weather and because I did not have any urgent tasks to solve, I chose to spend most of the next day comfortably in the officers' mess, among other things watching a film on the large screen. Pure luxury.

The next day I woke up to learn that three of *Esbern Snare*'s crew members had been robbed during a night on the town. This caused quite the upheaval on board, but it soon turned out that the guys had been careless in their dealings with the locals, to say the least. I felt that the matter was not serious enough for me to involve the local authorities in town. We had a really good relationship with them, and I did not want the three imprudent blokes', admittedly unpleasant, experience to jeopardise this relationship. What they had gone through is what we call building experience as a seaman. You learn something, but also, in this case, lose several thousands of kroner.

On 3 February *Esbern Snare* set out to sea, where we were expecting a visit from the Cypriot Minister of Foreign Affairs, Ioannis Kasoulides. He was a nice, older chap, and the visit was a success. The personal relations we established under such a visit proved very useful when we had to get diplomatic permission to dock in Limassol with short notice.

That day I also moved the force's operation area further to the south and thus closer to Cyprus. This would make it easier for us to get personnel and spare parts to and from the ships. It also gave *Esbern Snare*, *Helge Ingstad* and *Montrose* a chance to lower their state of readiness slightly, as it increased the warning time in the event that anyone on land launched a missile at the ships, for example. This lower state of readiness would help us save combat power for when we would actually need it.

As we moved the operation area, we also changed tactics: Now the units would take turns patrolling the area to the northeast outside Latakia. The objective was both to show that we were ready to move (which the Russians had previously argued that we were not) and to maintain an overview of the Pattern of Life in the area.

3 February was also the day when I noted in my journal for the first time that I was beginning to feel fatigued. My patience had grown thinner, and I was becoming angry more easily now. I decided to keep to myself for a bit to prevent this irritation from rubbing off on members of the crew. As supreme force commander, it was my job to keep the flag flying, and that required more of me these days. I was so damn tired of being a pawn in the strategic game of the Syrians and Russians, and in the next few days I had to work hard to keep up my spirits and morale.

The next day we had to return to Cyprus, as another deckhand had to go home. Her mother's flat had burned down and she therefore – quite understandably – had to return home to support her mother.

These days the press was saturated with rumours of an alleged pickup of chemical agents, but we received no official information from the OPCW or others. At the same time, the US tried to speed up the process, among other things by stating that a military solution was still a possibility if the Syrians failed to live up to their agreement with the OPCW and the UN. The Americans were clearly tired of waiting. They had provided the Syrians with a lot of equipment – including lorries for transporting the chemical agents – but only received complaints that the lorries were inoperable, probably because the Syrians did not know how to maintain them properly. A lot of the equipment had now been left unused for months, and as a consequence, it did not work when they finally wanted to use it. And oddly, despite the Syrians having so far been able to move the chemical agents around without problems during the more than two-year-long conflict, this now was suddenly unsafe. Clearly, they were stalling for time.

We spent the afternoon of 3 February practising Naval Gun Fire Support (NGFS). This involves shooting at a target on land with the fire being directed by a so-called spotter. However, in this case the shooting was directed at a target at sea, and we used the ship's helicopter for spotting. The exercise was a success, and we were ready to defend ourselves this way if necessary. Following the NGFS exercise, we conducted so-called throw-off firing: a shooting exercise where the ships use each other as targets. Helge Ingstad *thus had to shoot at us, and we had to shoot at them. We did not shoot directly at each other, however, as the ships' weapons systems had been adjusted to ensure that our grenades landed approx. 1,000 metres next to the Norwegian frigate. The photo shows the Norwegian frigate firing its 76-milimetre cannon. (S. Rudi/Forsvaret.no)*

At the same time, the Russians had sent another naval force to the area. This time the Russian Navy's only aircraft carrier, *Admiral Kuznetsov*, was approaching the area together with the destroyer *Admiral Levochenko* and a number of support vessels. *Admiral Levochenko* arrived in the area on 5 February followed by *Admiral Kuznetsov* and the rest of the force a couple of days later.

While waiting for news, we received a visit from the Danish Chief of Defence, General Peter Bartram, on 6 February. This was no mere social call, so we had put together a long programme that comprised the grand tour, dinner, briefing and a general-quarters drill, including toxic gas exercises that continued until well after midnight. The next morning the

Denmark's Chief of Defence, General Peter Bartram, speaking to the crew on Esbern Snare.

general observed a second Naval Gun Fire Support exercise from *Esbern Snare*'s helicopter before he was dropped off in Cyprus and we went off to patrol the Syrian coast to make our presence known and to establish a Pattern of Life picture.

Later that day we were informed that a new shipment would arrive in Latakia on 9 or 10 February. Just like last time, I had my military linguist call *Pyotr Velikiy* to, as agreed, share the information with them. Once again, the Russians clearly had not been informed by their own authorities, which was odd. Why did they have to rely on getting the information from us? The Russian Deputy Foreign Minister, Gennady Gatilov, made a short press statement to say that the next shipment would be large, which we were happy to hear. Unfortunately, our joy was short-lived, as we received a message from the OPCW stating that we should expect to collect 13-17 containers, which by no means could be said to constitute a large shipment.

Once again, we were surprised to see that the Syrians could get away with delaying the operation. At the tactical level, however, all I could do was put pressure on the OPCW and stress that the situation was unsat-

At our morning meeting on 9 February, we decided to send Esbern Snare's *helicopter to an area northeast of Cyprus to locate the Russian aircraft carrier, which we expected was anchored there.* Admiral Kuznetsov *was and still is Russia's only aircraft carrier, and our pilots were pleased to receive a mission with such a rare objective. Our helicopter did manage to locate the carrier and took some amazing pictures of a Russian Replenishment at Sea operation, among other things. The Russians go about this very differently than we do, and it was therefore very interesting. In the right-hand side of the photo is the Russian destroyer,* Admiral Levchenko.

isfactory to me, as I had five ships off the coast of Syria and several hundred personnel whose motivation I did not want to tax and whose lives I did not wish to endanger unnecessarily.

Taiko *and* Ark Futura *in the port of Latakia on 10 February 2014.*

The Third Pickup

On 10 February we conducted the third pickup. We loaded 13 containers, and the operation was characterised by coordination, a high level of security, procedures, new information and a high state of readiness etc. Once again, several containers had to be repackaged before they could be loaded onto *Taiko* and *Ark Futura*, but we made sure this had been pointed out and completed before we docked, so the two cargo ships did not have to wait for three to four hours in exposed positions. Despite our preparations, the operation took a long time. Yet everything went according to plan and the Moscow Agreement.

Having loaded the containers, we headed towards Limassol, where we had to pick up fuel for *Ark Futura* and *Taiko*. On the way we learned that the Joint Movement Transportation Organization (JMTO) under the Danish Defence, tasked with providing us with all kinds of logistics support from back home in Karup, had failed to procure the necessary authorisation from the Cypriot authorities to enter Cypriot waters with the two cargo ships. It was the same authority which, during the first pickup, had ordered the container off *Ark Futura* immediately after it had been loaded because the paperwork was not in order. Therefore, the JMTO was somewhat in 'bad standing' with me, and that night I sent a direct complaint to the Naval Command. Unfortunately, the episode left us doubting whether the logistical support back home really understood what was going on down here in the mission area. This was another example of the great distance in geography and mentality between Denmark and our location in the eastern Mediterranean. I had my staff call our ambassador in Cyprus, who promised to provide the necessary authorisation. Nonetheless, we did not manage to receive authorisation to move fuel, water and other provisions from Limassol out to the two waiting cargo ships. This was extremely frustrating, as *Ark Futura*'s fuel supply was now so low that if it did not refuel soon, it would not be safe to let the ship continue to pick up shipments in Latakia.

The next day we managed to refuel *Taiko*, but as we still had not received the necessary authorisation from the Cypriot authorities, we had to give up the idea of refuelling *Ark Futura* this time around. This meant that if a new shipment arrived in Latakia for pickup, I would have to divide the force and leave *Esbern Snare* in Limassol to look after *Ark Futura*, while the rest of the force left for Latakia. This was not an optimal situation, and I therefore had to send another trenchant signal to Naval Command, regretting the situation I was in due to the lack of timely attention on the part of the JMTO.

'Fortunately', the Syrian authorities informed us that afternoon that we were unlikely to receive more shipments until the beginning of March at the earliest. The reason, according to the Syrians, was that some of the chemical agents had been packed in barrels that subsequently turned out to be of too poor a quality. The substances therefore had to be repackaged, which would take a couple of days or weeks. Once again, the Syrians managed to delay the operation, and all we could do was receive the information and adapt to the situation.

We spent the following days trying to secure authorisation to refuel *Ark Futura* and on meetings with Dutch UN diplomat Sigrid Kaag. We received authorisation after some time and were finally able to refuel the ship via a tanker, which then sailed from Limassol and out into international waters, anchored next to *Ark Futura* and provided the necessary fuel. Before the meeting with Sigrid Kaag, I was asked to provide a list of topics for discussion. A couple of days earlier, I had sent a long signal to the OPCW containing all my frustrations and a couple of ideas for how we, with advantage, could and should do things differently in the future. In this connection, I had deliberately made use of the fact that I, as the operational commander on site, had a level of insight into the operation that would be difficult to argue against. I was thus able to get away with pointing out problems caused by the way the OPCW did things. At the same time, though, I was aware that I had to be balanced: If I was too 'shrill', this would shift focus away from my points of criticism, which especially concerned the lack of a timetable for the rest of the mission and the fact that I, for security reasons, wanted to collect as large amounts of chemical agents as possible on each run to avoid calling into port in Latakia too many times. During the meeting, I sensed that Sigrid Kaag was under pressure, as the quick results – which a lot of people had expected to see before the operation began – still had not materialised. She was unable to provide a timetable for the remaining pickups or to accommodate my wish to reduce the number of calls into port. I therefore had to be satisfied with informing the OPCW management of my

The crew on Esbern Snare *photographed together with representatives of the Danish Emergency Management Agency, the Danish tax authority (SKAT) and the Danish Frogman Corps, among others. In the background are Blue Ghost and two of the Danish Frogman Corps' dinghies.*

challenges, and all I could do now was hope that they would be able to accommodate my wishes at some point in the future.

After the meeting with Sigrid Kaag I took some half days off. My wife, Kirsten, had travelled to Cyprus, and we spent the next five days together. Even though Kirsten was there, I participated in the daily meetings on board *Esbern Snare* and monitored the signal traffic to remain 100 per cent up to date on situational developments, but fortunately I also had time to relax and do a bit of sightseeing in Cyprus. It was a much-needed break and very hard to say goodbye to Kirsten when she had to return home.

On 18 February, I was back under full steam on *Esbern Snare*. During the morning meeting at 08:00, I learned that there had been an episode that night with some small Egyptian boats, possibly fishermen or cigarette smugglers who had ventured a bit too close to *Taiko* and *Ark Futura* in the holding area between Cyprus and Syria. *Helge Ingstad*, which had been in front that night, had responded first by issuing warnings over

Prime Minister Helle Thorning-Schmidt being interviewed for the news by the Danish Broadcasting Corporation (DR) on the deck of Esbern Snare.

the radio, and when that had failed, it had fired three star shells and a series of shots with the ship's signal gun. This had made the boats change course and leave.

This episode made me, together with my staff, look into how best to respond in such situations. The commander of the Norwegian frigate had as such reacted the way he should, but I still felt that he had been a bit too aggressive. If instead he had chosen to start by moving *Helge Ingstad*, all he had to do was watch whether this also made the small boats change course and continue to head towards the frigate. If they did, they were likely to have hostile intentions; if they merely continued along the previous course and at the same speed, they probably did not constitute a threat, and we could have avoided using star shells, raising the state of readiness and the actual danger of firing shots. I chose not to voice my criticism of the frigate's commander, however, as I did not wish to 'micromanage' my ship captains. They should be free to act in accordance with the orders I had already given.

During her visit, the Prime Minister seemed relaxed, inquisitive and interested. She gave a great speech to the staff. And all in all, the visit was a success, giving me the impression that she and the civil service learned a lot about the operation and about the Navy. (K. Navntoft/Scanpix)

On 19 February *Esbern Snare* received a visit from then Danish Prime Minister, Helle Thorning-Schmidt, and the Cypriot President, Nicos Anastasiades. The aim of the Prime Minister's visit was to show her support for the mission, and she brought along a host of reporters. Two heads of state in a small ship meant a busy day, where I – along with the rest of the crew – was constantly answering questions, adjusting plans and doing everything else that goes along with such a VIP visit.

The day after the PM's visit, my Norwegian Deputy Commander and I visited the French destroyer *Cassard*, which was in the area and whose commander wanted to treat us to lunch and a chat about the operation. It was good fun, and the French naval officer had a lot of questions.

At the end of February, we noticed a change in the way the Russian cruiser *Pyotr Velikiy* was operating around us. It began to follow us more closely, often so close that it looked like part of our force. Perhaps it was because the Russian intelligence ship, which had been following us

The RECSYR force photographed from the air on 20 February 2014. Leading the way is Esbern Snare *followed by* Ark Futura *and* Taiko. *In the foreground* Montrose *and in the background* Helge Ingstad.

closely up until then, had docked in Cyprus, or perhaps it was to support the strategic announcement that Russia was protecting the cargo ships. We did not know. Naturally, when in international waters we had let the Russians manoeuvre as they saw fit, but the development worried us slightly. If we found ourselves in a situation resembling the one with the Egyptian boats the other night, we could not be sure that the Russians would react in the same – after all – restrained way as the Norwegians. If the Russians sank an innocent, civilian vessel, the press could easily make it look as if we had a part in this. But there was nothing we could do to change this.

That Saturday we paid the floating refuelling station, USNS *Walter S. Diehl*, another visit. As always, the American supply ship was ready to service us, and this ensured a high degree of flexibility. Both *Esbern Snare* and *Montrose* refuelled, whereas the commander of *Helge Ingstad* did not wish to conduct a RAS operation that day.

Later that day, 22 February, *Montrose* had to leave the force and return to Great Britain. In that connection I had asked the commander of the frigate permission to come on board the ship for a farewell visit. My Norwegian Deputy Commander and I sailed to *Montrose*, where we spoke to the commander of the ship for about an hour. Commander

The crew on Montrose *when the ship left Operation RECSYR. Montrose was replaced by the British destroyer* Diamond, *which arrived in Limassol the day* Montrose *left for Great Britain.*

Parkin told us that participating in Operation RECSYR had been the most rewarding experience in his time as commander, since removing chemical agents from Syria had really made sense. It was the first time ever that a British unit had been under Danish command, and in his view this had been a success. His praise made me feel proud, I must admit.

To conclude the visit, I made a speech to the crew who had assembled on the frigate's helicopter deck. I commended their professional approach to the task and thanked them for their hard work. I admitted that we had picked up far fewer containers than we had expected and hoped for at this point, but that we should still be pleased with the few we had collected, as the chemical agents now could not be used against civilians in Syria.

We then returned to *Esbern Snare* with the gifts we had received from the commander: a *Montrose* cap and a nice ashtray made from the bottom part of a shell casing. The latter was a particularly nice gift, seeing as it had been made on board and had been completed at 02:00 the night before our visit.

Later that night I received a signal saying that there was every indication that we could pick up one or even two shipments in Latakia the following week.

I hereby certify that *[name]* has participated in Operation Removal of Chemical Agents from Syria (OPRECSYR). This operation is the maritime part of the transport of chemical agents away from Syria and it is done in support of the Organization for the Prohibition of Chemical Weapon/United Nations Joint Mission for the destruction chemical weapons that is mandated by United Nations Security Council Resolution 2118.

The Maritime transport of the chemical agents was conducted on board M/V Taiko and M/V Ark Futura. The two cargo ships were escorted by warships from Norway, United Kingdom and Denmark. You participated as a part of the crew on M/V Taiko.

Each individual participating in this operation has contributed to making the world a safer place. The removal of the chemical agents from Syrian means that these agents can never again be used against innocent people. You have been an important part of the removal of the chemical agents from Syria. Without your support it would not have been possible.

You have taken on the responsibility in this significant operation and have acted in a highly professional manner – you can be proud of your footprint in this historic event.

Signed

TORBEN MIKKELSEN
Commodore
Commander Task Group 420.01

Not only the crew on the war ships showed their support of the operation. I realised that the civilians on the cargo ships were also very proud of participating in the operation. They felt that they contributed to world peace, which was almost moving. Subsequently, we therefore gave each of the civilian crew members on the cargo ships a letter like the one above, detailing the purpose of the mission and expressing my gratitude for the work of the crew member in question.

This sounded right, but I must admit that I was a bit sceptical as to whether it was really true, considering the development these past couple of weeks.

On 23 February, in order to demonstrate my desire for friendly relations and cooperation with the Russians, I had my military linguist call my Russian colleague to wish him a happy 'Defender of the Fatherland Day' – a state holiday in Russia, where the population may show their gratitude to those serving in the Russian Armed Forces. Once again, I thus hoped to establish a good relationship with the commander of the Russian cruiser and thereby facilitate cooperation. I also took this opportunity to inform the Russians that we had learned that a shipment might arrive for pickup in Latakia the following week, and I promised to share with them as soon as possible any specific information I might receive.

On 24 February Blue Ghost once again flew to the north side of Cyprus to see what the Russian aircraft carrier was doing. All in all, it left us with the impression that Admiral Kuznetsov *was a bit of a 'paper tiger', whose main purpose was to show its presence in the area. This was unlike the planes belonging to other nations overflying our ships. They would fly over us at a high altitude and always make sure to engage their Identify Friend or Foe (IFF) systems as they approached us to show they that were friendly. They took their work very seriously. They knew that our weapons systems were loaded and ready and that they ought not impose on us a situation of uncertainty in which we were unable to identify them and therefore would open fire.*

On 24 February we received a signal saying that the next shipment would be ready for pickup in Latakia two days later. The contents of the shipment were unclear, though, and we thus had to wait for more information before we could decide whether to call into port with *Ark Futura* or *Taiko*. I immediately called *Diamond* and *Helge Ingstad* out to sea. They were both waiting in Limassol and had not planned to sail out until 24 hours later, but I needed them now, and they set to work immediately. It was an important strategic signal to send, i.e. that all the participating nations were ready.

The same afternoon we received a new plan from the OPCW, which had finally managed to get the Syrians to draw up a timetable for the rest of the operation. According to the plan, all the Syrian storage sites, except for two, had to be emptied by 13 April at the latest. The last two could probably be emptied by 27 April. This was good news, even though the

The British destroyer, Diamond, *protecting* Ark Futura, *which at this point was carrying quite a lot of containers on open deck. (MoD)*

plan involved calling into port in Latakia three times a week up until mid-April, and we would, after weeks of waiting, suddenly have a lot on our slate now.

If everyone stuck to the plan, we would be able to transfer the first-priority agents to *Cape Ray* on 1 or 2 May. Even though this meant that we would not be able to complete the mission by June, as the hydrolysis process on *Cape Ray* would take more than 30 days, it did not change the fact that this plan was the most positive piece of news we had received for weeks. Now all we had to do was keep our fingers crossed and hope that everyone stuck to the plan.

However, regardless of the new Syrian plan, the OPCW once again did not manage to inform us of the exact time of the pickup on 26 February and the contents of the shipment. Our liaison officer therefore called the OPCW staff in Latakia after midnight, and only then did we receive the information we needed to start planning the operation.

They informed us that the next day's shipment included 20 tons of mustard gas. That is, a ready-mixed, liquid warfare agent, the lethal dose of which was as little as 0.4 grams – and we had to collect containers of barrels containing up to 1,000 litres each. We would have to be careful not to rock the boat!

If we managed to load 20 tons, there would be no more mustard gas left in Syria, as far as we were informed. The shipment was therefore given high priority, and it constituted an important strategic signal.

26 February

This was the day when we would be carrying the most highly profiled shipment out of the country. We cleared the timetable with the Russians last night, and everything went well – that is, right until the Syrians informed us that they had to add extra armour plating to the containers on the very same day of the pickup. Why the hell did not they do this yesterday instead of today? This has caused a delay of one and a half hours. We have now informed all the units, and that is not easy considering the many languages involved. And that was not all. I have just been told that the extra armour appears to have destroyed the GPS transmitter and the Anti Tampering Device (which is the security device that reveals whether or not anyone has tampered with the shipment after it left the OPCW inspection and before it arrived in Latakia, where OPCW personnel are present).

We asked the OPCW several weeks ago whether they were certain that the extra armour would not affect this equipment, and their response was: 'Oh, of course not'. They had everything under control. My ass. Pardon my French. So, now the OPCW wants me to decide whether the containers can be loaded even though this has not been fixed.

Of course, I cannot accept this. It is their responsibility to provide secure containers. They are responsible for this aspect, regardless of whether this means that we have to leave without the containers. I certainly did not invent the Anti Tampering Device; they did. And if it does not work, they can drive the lorries themselves if they are afraid someone might add something to the containers which does not belong there. Well, I am sorry, but I am getting really tired of this. So, we just have to wait some more – all seven ships and around 1,400 people – because someone does not take their job seriously and messes up.

I believe my frustration with the Syrians' constant (and partially successful) attempts to stall for time is evident from the above excerpt from my journal. We did manage to pick up the mustard gas, though, and we suddenly found ourselves in a situation where our main challenge was the fact that these pickups had become routine. One pickup now began to follow another, and we were developing a routine where we would call into Limassol for supplies in between pickups before returning to the waters off Latakia. I therefore impressed on the force via may staff that they had to remember that we were operating in a land affected by civil war with a lot of weapons and explosives in circulation, and we did not know who controlled these. We did not know the motives of the various actors in this complex land of ethnic tensions, tribal cultures, dozens of rebel forces, government troops and the personal army of al-Assad – a patchwork of actors waging war on each other, and we did not have an overview of their individual agendas.

With the third pickup a success and the force in safety under the Mediterranean sun, I once again had time to consider what to do when *Esbern Snare* was to be relieved in May. We had decided that the support ship would be replaced by the frigate *Peter Willemoes*, which required some planning between us and the authorities back home.

That day my Norwegian Deputy Commander and I once again visited the new British contribution to the mission: the brand-new Type 45 destroyer, *Diamond*. We took off in Blue Ghost but had only covered a

A Syrian lorry driving a container containing chemical agents on board Ark Futura.

couple of hundred metres when the observer announced that the airspeed indicator was not working properly. The indicator provides input for a lot of instruments, and you cannot fly without it, so the helicopter was brought down again. Instead, I was transferred to *Diamond* via *Esbern Snare*'s dinghy.

I was excited to visit the highly sophisticated British destroyer. It is an air defence destroyer equipped with really good sensors and weapons systems, and it constituted a huge capacity to our mission. It was great knowing that one of the latest and most capable air-defence units in the world was part of my force. The visit was a success, and we had a good talk with Commander Andrew Ingham. *Diamond* was clearly ready for the operation!

We returned to *Esbern Snare* on Blue Ghost, which had been repaired in the meantime, and news of the next shipment was waiting for us. It was a second-priority shipment for *Taiko*, which would be ready for us the following day. The plan we had recently received from the OPCW really appeared to work, and we could thus look forward to collecting another shipment in Latakia in three or four days.

As usual, we called the Russians to provide them with the time of the pickup and details of the shipment. They were very grateful, because once again their own authorities had failed to inform them. Nevertheless, they subsequently behaved as though they had been the ones informing us of the pickup and as if it was their job to tell us what to do. A strange situation, which was probably a result of the fact that Moscow continued to tell them to act as coordinator and commander. This did not change anything, though. We coordinated the operation with the Russians and Chinese, and we had the cargo chips, and without them there would be no pickup. As far as I was concerned, the Russians were free to feel and act as though they were the ones that did the coordinating; what mattered to me was picking up shipments. Moreover, it was probably more important for my Russian colleague to demonstrate leadership and coordination power to Moscow than it was for me to assert my position. What mattered was collecting the shipments safely and quickly.

We had planned to dock in Limassol to bring new supplies on board and to allow the crew a chance to stretch their legs on land, but that plan had to be abandoned. There was a general strike in Limassol, and we feared that it would delay our replenishment to the extent that we would not be able to return to Latakia in time for the next shipment. This change of plans was cause for a somewhat strained atmosphere on board. Several crew members had invited their family to Cyprus and hoped to be able to spend time with them in connection with our call into port – and now they might not even get a chance to see them. They had been aware of the risk, but I nevertheless felt bad for those affected.

On 28 February *Taiko* collected 10 containers of second-priority material. Before entering the port of Latakia, however, we had to open one of the containers containing mustard gas already on the deck of *Ark Futura*. The door to the container had not been closed properly, and the container therefore was not tight. We documented the opening with pictures and text, and resealed it. We also took pictures inside the container, which showed that the Syrians' packaging in fact appeared proficient. The 1,000-litre metal containers holding the gas had been secured with chains. And as we were dealing with dangerous warfare agents, ready for use, it was good to see that they had been properly secured.

Once again, the pickup was delayed. This time we were informed that the convoys transporting the chemical agents had been attacked on their way to Latakia. The OPCW personnel in Latakia therefore had to inspect the vehicles and containers etc., looking for visible signs of fire. However, I suspected that this was simply another attempt to delay the transport as much as possible. The affair also turned out to be storm in a teacup, which had been started by the Russian liaison officers on board *Helge Ingstad*. They claimed that they had learned about the attack in the media, but it turned out to be old news from 27 January, with which we were familiar. And the containers we had picked up on 28 January also looked perfectly unharmed, as they in fact were.

We did experience an episode while loading the containers, as one of the gas meters mounted in the port suddenly showed a reading. Such a reading might indicate a spill from one of the containers, and naturally it had to be checked out before the rest of the containers could be loaded. The procedure in case of a suspected spill was that everything had to be checked and removed from the containers, which had to be cleaned and prepared with new cat litter on the floor (we used cat litter due to its high absorbency in case of minor spills). Not until the containers had been cleaned and reloaded with the chemical agents could they be taken on board *Taiko*. This was quite a hassle, and we were relieved to hear that a thorough inspection had showed no spillage but merely evaporation, probably caused by a thread on one of the lids which was not 100 per cent clean. After 10 hours in Latakia, we were able to put out to sea again. We left the port at 23:30, the fourth pickup successfully completed.

The next day we learned that the OPCW had sent out a tweet saying that the pickup had been completed before ships and crew had even left Latakia. I was annoyed to hear this, because calling into Latakia was not without its dangers. For security reasons, we operated with a high level of operational security and did not allow e.g. civilian phone and Internet use during pickups, just as we minimised all communication with external actors until we were outside reach of the coast. The OPCW mission headquarters in Cyprus had undermined all of this with their tweet. I asked our liaison officer in Cyprus to inform the OPCW that I as commander of the force was displeased and that I did not expect this to repeat.

After the fourth pickup, we had to go to Limassol for fresh supplies. While in port, we had time for another visit from back home, this time from the Director of SKAT (Denmark's tax agency), Jørgen Rønnow Simonsen, who wanted to pay the members of his staff manning the transportable scanner a visit. The Director and one of the platoon leaders were briefed about the mission and given a tour of the ship.

The next day we received a similar visit from the commander of the Engineer Regiment, who was the superior of the Army's seven chemical specialists from Skive Barracks on board *Esbern Snare*. That day a lot of my staff returned home, and I therefore spent a lot of time welcoming their replacements and giving them a mission status update. These were busy days.

At 23:30 on 2 March, we once again left Limassol bound for Latakia, where we would be picking up another shipment the following day – this time of a size that required calling into port with both *Taiko* and *Ark Futura*. Therefore, the entire force was involved, just as we coordinated the operation with the Russians and Chinese.

3 March

We will be picking up eight containers: three containing one of the main components for nerve gas and five with a main component for the very dangerous nerve gas, sarin. The latter will be provided in the original 2,000-litre steel containers from the 1980s. Our cargo is beginning to contain the more dangerous agents, and the safety distance in case of a spill in Latakia is approx. 2.5 kilometres. We therefore keep a close eye on the wind speed and direction in connection with pickups. It is vital to how we position *Esbern Snare* and our rubber dinghies inside the port, enabling them to support *Ark Futura* and *Taiko*. Luckily for us – but perhaps less so for the residents of Latakia – the wind has changed direction inland, which has allowed us the highest degree of flexibility possible in connection with the operation.

As always, the Syrians do not seem to prepare for a pickup. Nevertheless, we transferred our liaison officers at 10:00. The GPS trackers tell us that the lorries are moving, and our calculations show that it will take them six hours to reach Latakia.

Everyone to their posts, general quarters at 12:45, as we prepare to arrive at 14:30. Everything is going according to plan and all the ships are informed and start to move. We must call into port with both *Ark Futura* and *Taiko*, which in logistical terms is no walk in the park.

We are suddenly informed of trouble with the shipment for *Ark Futura*. The GPS trackers tell us that one of five lorries has stopped at some kind of farm 30-40 metres from the motorway to Latakia. We do not know what has happened; it could be an accident or something suspicious. Time passes, and the lorry turns out to have a flat tyre. I have already considered the possibility of punctures, but have not been able to do anything, as this is clearly a Syrian matter. The lorries move at more than 100 kilometres per hour, and they are very heavy due to the cargo and not least the armour plating. Of course, the tyres heat up, and then they explode. This also happened last time. It is a bit odd really that the drivers are not keener about preventing accidents, seeing as they are moving 6,000 litres of one of the main components for nerve gas.

At 20:30, *Ark Futura* left the port of Latakia, another successful and not least safe pickup completed. ☺ Though I am still not content with the manner in which we have to coordinate with the lorries on land.

The Russian Annexation of the Crimea

On 4 March the crew on *Helge Ingstad* was relieved, and the approx. 130 new crew members were given a so-called running start, as we would be picking up a shipment in Latakia the following day. We had planned for *Ark Futura* to receive the next shipment, though, which meant that *Helge Ingstad* would not have to enter the port, where the risk level after all was somewhat higher. We also sent my Norwegian Deputy Commander to the frigate to act as a kind of consultant during their first pickup.

All of this was overshadowed by developments at the strategic level. For some time now, the conflict concerning the Crimea had been smouldering. The peninsula officially belonged to Ukraine, though the main city of Sevastopol housed the headquarters of the Russian Black Sea Fleet. In February 2014, riots broke out in Sevastopol, among other places, and at the end of the month a large number of unidentified soldiers – equipped with Russian weapons and equipment – took control of the peninsula.

This was met with massive protests from the Western world, as Russia in several treaties back in the 1990s had guaranteed Ukraine's territorial sovereignty. The Danish Government was among the countries that criticised the Russians' behaviour. Naturally, I supported my Government in this, but it left me in a situation where I had spent a lot of resources establishing a good working relationship with my Russian counterparts. All this now risked going down like a lead balloon.

This development meant that almost all cooperation between NATO and Russia was suspended. It also affected Operation RECSYR, as Russia at the end of January had suggested that the Russian ships under the auspices of the NATO/Russian Council cooperation should participate in the protection of *Cape Ray*, while it destroyed the Syrian first-priority agents at sea. This no longer seemed like a realistic solution. Obviously, I had no influence on events concerning the Crimea and the relationship between NATO and Russia. All I could do was hope that the personal relationship I had built with the Russians on *Pyotr Velikiy* would prevent the cooperative effort from breaking down completely. The development meant that I had to impress on the ships in the force that we would continue to act as hitherto, regardless of the international crisis – that is, we would continue as if nothing had happened. I felt certain that the Russians were keeping a close eye on us to see if events on the Crimea would change things; they would not. We had a job to do, regardless of what happened in the Black Sea.

5 March
Another pickup day is here. We are about to collect 36,000 litres of the main component for the nerve gas VX, enough to kill around 22 million people. We have begun to focus more on the gas threat of a potential leak. The safety distance is 2,400 metres, and we must make sure not to be sailing upwind, i.e., against the wind direction.

Liaison officers from the Russian flagship were transferred at 10:00. These are the same guys who have been here during the last pickups. They are good guys, really, and very humble and friendly. We set out and everything went according to plan. Several ships and more than 1,000 people were heading for Syria – and then, once again, we were informed of trouble with one of the vehicles! So, the entire force had to turn around and head out to sea again. Three hours later we could call into port again. This time everything went by the book. Our procedures and communications now work perfectly, and when we finally arrived, we were able to move quickly. It took us little more than an hour to pick up the 36,000 litres of chemical substances.

On 6 March it was my turn to pay the Chinese frigate, *Yancheng*, an official visit. It had been some time since I had received the invitation, but I had had to wait for the right moment, both concerning pickups in Latakia and the developments at the strategic level.

We were set to arrive at 10:00, and exactly on time Blue Ghost landed on the deck of the Chinese frigate. It was the first time ever that a Danish helicopter landed on a Chinese warship. The ship's photographers were waiting for us and took a lot of pictures before I even managed to get out of the helicopter. I was received by the ship's commanding officer and guided around an extremely clean – almost sterile – ship. Perfectly clean walls with Chinese posters of large hosts of soldiers marching and some

Meeting on the Chinese frigate.

screens, which in a matter of minutes showed my picture and read 'Welcome Admiral Mikkelsen'.

We were led into a conference room, where I spent an hour drinking green tea and talking to the Chinese commander. Our conversation left me with the impression that the Chinese, just like the Russians, had no knowledge of the further developments of the operation. They knew nothing about the OPCW's plans, and the commander was clearly fishing for more information. However, I still did not want to be too frank with them, since if the Russians learned that I had told the Chinese something they did not know, they might consider it an attempt on my part to act as the supreme coordinator, seeking to drive a wedge between Russia and China. And that was the last thing I wanted to do.

At the same time, though, our success depended on the Chinese and Russians' ability to fulfil the aspects of the operation we had agreed on in the Moscow Plan, so I had to carefully indicate to the Chinese that we might soon need their help in the waters outside Latakia. They seemed relieved to receive the small crumbs of information I was able to give them, and I could understand why. Just like me, they had to have a plan. Operating a ship without knowing when you will get a chance to collect fresh supplies, for example, is not easy.

After the meeting, we exchanged the obligatory gifts. We gave them a copy of *Esbern Snare*'s coat of arms, caps with the ship's logo and a bottle

I had expected a stiff and very formal meeting on board Yancheng, *and I was not disappointed. However, the Chinese were very friendly, and the meeting had a positive effect on our continued cooperation. The photo shows the Chinese commander receiving* Esbern Snare's *coat of arms.*

of Dr. Nielsen (a Danish bitter). I was then given a tour of the ship that was so clean you might have suspected it of never having been used, which was consistent with the fact that we had at no point during our time in the Mediterranean seen them fire their weapons or do anything else that might dirty a warship …

The tour was very extensive and included facilities which I would not have thought the Chinese wished to share with us. For example, we visited the frigate's CIC and saw its weapons and all the equipment on open deck. During the tour, the ship's photographers continued to take dozens of pictures, and when we reached the bridge – where all personnel stood at attention while I was present – I was suddenly presented with a huge visitors' book (50 x 40 centimetres) and asked to 'write something for the crew'. Now, that I had not prepared for, but apparently I did well, because when my greeting was translated into Chinese everyone on the bridge clapped their hands for a long time …

When we reached the aft deck, where *Yancheng*'s helicopter was ready on display, Chinese national television suddenly wanted to do an interview! Another thing I had not been informed of beforehand, but I could hardly refuse. Fortunately, the reporter was kind and only asked easy questions.

Signing the visitors' book.

Then we had lunch consisting of 18 dishes to be eaten with chopsticks. After lunch I asked to say hello to the chef. I do not think they had expected this, but he appeared wearing his chef's hat, and I got up to shake his hand and thank him for dinner – and to give him one of our sleeve labels. When we left the officers' mess shortly afterwards, I also shook the hands of all the waiters. I do not think they are used to that either.

I had been given a Chinese Velcro sleeve label by the Chinese commander. As we made our way to the aft deck, I attached it to my uniform on the chest to show my appreciation. I told him that I was now wearing the official People's Liberation Army Navy label closest to my heart as a symbol of our friendship.

I left *Yancheng* in *Esbern Snare*'s dinghy, feeling that the visit, all things considered, had been very successful.

On 7 March we were informed that the pickup plan the Syrians had drawn up at the end of February was not realisable after all. This was annoying because it undermined our ability to plan ahead. The problem was still that the ships had to call into Limassol once in a while to pick up fresh supplies, new crew members or the like. And without a plan for the remaining pickups in Latakia, there was a risk that one or more of our units would be in Cyprus, unable to reach Latakia in time. The ships, after all, were not dominos that you could move to the desired location

Interview with Chinese national television – now wearing my Chinese ball cap.

at short notice. All we could do, though, was take the news into consideration and hope that it would not affect the remaining pickups.

Shortly afterwards we were informed that the next shipment had been postponed for 24 hours but that the subsequent pickups would not be affected by this. Once again, I was very frustrated by the Syrians' behaviour. I knew that I could not let my frustration shine through, though, as I constantly had the attention of 600 crew members. Everyone close to me paid attention to my mood and listened to what I said and did. You have to act accordingly, and I thus had to show both motivation and commitment – not act stupidly or naïvely.

Esbern Snare *and* Ark Futura *practise transferring supplies, e.g. food, to* Ark Futura. *We had to be able to transfer supplies to the cargo ship, even if we, due to technical errors, were prevented from using the dinghy or the helicopter. However,* Ark Futura *did not have the equipment for such a transfer, which in the Navy is known as a Light Jackstay. Some clever fellows on* Esbern Snare *had taken a very pragmatic approach to the problem, though, and created a solution involving ropes, pulleys and a large group of people acting as the human elastic stretching the line used for the transfer of supplies. Finally, they attached a large pallet truck as a base on* Ark Futura, *which of course was not prepared for a manoeuvre of this kind. As evident from the photos, it worked.*

Crew members watching the port of Latakia closely from the open bridge on Esbern Snare.

Rocket Attack

9 March
Finally, we are ready for the next pickup. We never received any explanation for why the pickup could not be completed yesterday. I think they have received and reacted to reports of possible attacks – which of course is the sensible thing to do.

Approximately one hour into the pickup, three rockets were observed hitting an area close to the port, and a couple of buildings nearby burst into flames. Someone in the city returned fire, shooting inland.

You could sense the nervousness on the radio, and I was suddenly informed of a possible missile attack, and the force very quickly went into high alert, focussing on so-called 'Air Threat Warning RED'. So far, I had stuck to the plan, namely, to continue with the pickup, as I had found that the opposition's chances of shooting into the city would take the form of a single, isolated attack, as this would reveal their firing position, forcing them to relocate to avoid Syrian counterattacks with planes and bombs. Consequently, since we had not been hit, there was very low likelihood of another attack. So, we hurried up and left the port as quickly as possible.

Furthermore, there was no indication that the rocket attacks had been directed at us. Most had hit a roundabout approx. two and a half kilometres from the port and approx. 700 metres from *Ark Futura* with a wayward hit (seen from the attacker's point of view), including one splash impact in the water inside the harbour. If we had been the target, they would not have missed – based on the fact that the majority of the shots had in fact hit the same area. However, when we received reports of indications of missile attacks in the works, I seriously considered aborting the pickup. This information came from the new crew on the Norwegian frigate, and as I felt that they might – understandably – feel more uncertain about the entire situation, and the threat assessment in particular, I asked about the credibility of this information. Fortunately, it turned out to be based on an erroneous interpretation of events. The crew on board the frigate had acted correctly, but I was pleased to learn that there was no threat after all. We switched to a lower state of air defence readiness and completed the pickup.

During and after the situation, I made an effort to calm everyone, as I could tell that people were too anxious. It is important to keep calm because panic can lead to erroneous information further intensifying the feeling of insecurity of those involved and thus the entire situation. Suddenly, people begin to speak more rapidly on the communication networks, which can make it difficult for the recipient to understand the message, forcing him to ask for the message to be repeated, and this is unfortunately counterproductive to security. I will address this in my signals today.

So far, we have received reports of three dead and 15-20 wounded Syrians, but as this information stems from open sources, its accuracy can be difficult to verify.

I subsequently recommended the Naval Command back home that we issue a press release about the incident, but neither the Danish nor Norwegian Navy's headquarters wanted to do this. Instead, they chose to be reactive and wait to see whether the media caught hold of the story themselves. In my opinion, this was not the right thing to do, as a simple Google search showed that the story had already gone viral and could even be found on Facebook. I worried about the families of the force's approx. 1,500 crew members, whom I did not want to see get upset from learning about the incident in the news before they had been told that everyone was safe. Moreover, not reporting the incident might cause someone to suspect us of not playing our cards face up in general. I told the Naval Command, but they stuck to their decision not to report the incident. My report for the day was therefore merely that the force had picked up the chemical agents in Latakia and that everything had gone according to plan.

While communicating with the Naval Command about the attack, we also invested a lot of resources trying to determine what had actually happened during the pickup. If the attack had in fact been directed at us,

News of the rocket attack was released by the Russian Ministry of Foreign Affairs on 13 March in the form of a press statement which suggested that the Danish/Norwegian naval force had been the actual target of the attack. Why this was suggested, I do not know, but it certainly supported the Russian story that the Syrian regime was innocent.

then we found ourselves in an entirely new and much more dangerous situation. However, the next day we concluded that there was every indication that the attack had been directed at al-Assad's forces in the city and not at us. Nevertheless, it meant that the pickup scheduled for 11 March had been postponed to the 13th to give al-Assad's forces time to make sure that the episode would not repeat.

Preparing cakes for the crew on Esbern Snare.

Home on Leave

For a long time, I had considered going home on a week's leave and had been trying to find a suitable time. I now decided to do this from 17 to 26 March. My Norwegian Deputy Commander would still be on the ship and thus able to take command while I was away. My superiors back home gave me the go-ahead, and I was thus able to inform Captain Kvalvaag and the rest of the staff of my decision. The next day was my birthday, and it was celebrated right from early morning. The commander of *Esbern Snare* had hinted that I should stay in my cabin until 07:15. And on the dot, the door was opened and in the passageway was the chaplain playing the birthday tune on the trumpet, while the commander and about ten other crew members who had also showed up sang along. I received some nice gifts and a delicious breakfast tray in my cabin. I also got a photo of the crew with their signatures, which made me very happy – a personal gift, which due to the writing cannot be put up anywhere, though. Other than this, it was business as usual, except for the cake at 15:00 to celebrate my and four other crew members' birthday.

At the beginning of March, I had invited the Russians for lunch on board *Esbern Snare* on 12 March. They did not reply to my invitation, though, probably due to the unresolved situation concerning the Crimea. We were not certain that they would respond at all – when we finally received confirmation on 11 March.

I had informed the Naval Command of the invitation but had deliberately not asked for permission to hold the meeting. I believed I was authorised to invite the Russians for lunch and that it did not have to be approved by my superiors back home. I was the man on the scene who knew the details of my relationship with the Russians best, and I felt that we should be able to meet and discuss the operation and our joint task. It was important for me to be able to look my Russian colleagues in the eye and show them that I wanted to continue our cooperation, regardless of events in other parts of the world and any restrictions regarding Russia's cooperation with NATO.

Less than 45 minutes before the Russians were expected to embark *Esbern Snare,* I received a signal from the Naval Command back home stressing that the meeting and all conversation with the Russians could only concern Operation RECSYR and not touch upon the situation in Ukraine or the Crimea.

I had already written to the Naval Command the day before that I only intended to discuss the present mission, and I therefore considered the signal unnecessary. But apparently the people in Aarhus had to be absolutely certain that I had been informed not to exceed my mandate and allow the Russians to raise the subject of the Crimea. However, the Russians never mentioned the Crimea, and the meeting turned out to be a both pleasant and constructive experience. I guess we had the same objective?

I had decided, in honour of the occasion, to serve beer for lunch. We usually never do this when at sea, but this was a unique situation, and it was important for me to create a relaxed atmosphere and demonstrate that regardless of what happened elsewhere we still had a joint task to fulfil.

Marathon on *Taiko* and Fire on *Ark Futura*

Immediately after the Russians had disembarked, I was transferred to *Taiko* where the crew had organised a 'chemical marathon'. Crew members from the five ships could sign up for a deck marathon, which involved running around the deck 105 times, corresponding to the 42 kilometres of an official marathon. The participants could either run the entire distance themselves or participate in teams of two or four and split the distance between them.

While I was on board *Taiko*, we suddenly saw *Esbern Snare* sail towards *Ark Futura* at high speed. I hurried onto the bridge and was informed that the cargo ship had caught fire. The crew on *Esbern Snare* had therefore called to general quarters and headed towards *Ark Futura* prepared to assist them and provide chemical and fire control.

The 'chemical marathon' was a great initiative that I wanted to support, and I therefore did a couple of laps with the Danish runners – wearing uniform and boots. (R.R. Nicolaisen)

The crew on *Ark Futura* soon managed to put out the fire without help, though, and could announce that everything was back to normal. Nevertheless, *Esbern Snare* remained on site for a couple of hours, among other things to monitor *Ark Futura* through an infrared camera capable of detecting heat generation, which would detect any heat generation that might rekindle the fire.

From on board *Taiko* the situation had appeared very serious with a huge plume of black smoke and reports that the fire was close to the containers with mustard gas. I was therefore subsequently transferred from *Taiko* to *Ark Futura* via *Esbern Snare*, as I wanted to go talk to the skipper to see whether he and the ship were okay. On board I met a completely calm skipper, who was on the bridge reporting the incident to the Danish Maritime Authority. The fire turned out to have started on the deck in two 20-litre metal buckets containing a bit of paint, as one of the crew members had emptied an ashtray into one of them. The buckets had stood about one and a half metres from the containers with mustard gas, so the situation could easily have turned grim. Subsequently, the containers were thoroughly examined but did not appear to have been damaged. Fortunately, we had practised scenarios like this one several times involving fire on the deck of the cargo ships, and we were pleased to see that the emergency procedures worked perfectly and that our training had borne fruit.

I sent a signal to the Naval Command about the incident and suggested that we – to pre-empt a potential rumour mill and to calm the families back home – posted a small notice on the incident on the Naval Command's website. They did not wish to do so, however, as they did not believe the incident was serious enough. I very much disagreed, as I considered it very important to keep the public informed of the events of the mission, both for good and bad. Whether the events were dramatic or not was less important. The important thing was to keep the public informed, as they might otherwise suspect concealment. This would affect our credibility, especially if incidents like this one came out in the end. If I had had a say in the matter, we would have announced that a couple of metal buckets on board *Ark Futura* had caught fire, and that nothing else had happened, aside from the fact that we had learned that our chemical and fire control procedures worked perfectly. This would have deflated potential later stories, but they saw things differently back home in Aarhus. And they did, after all, have the final say in the matter.

On 13 March the British destroyer, *Diamond*, received a delegation from the British Government and the British military. The distinguished visitors included the Minister of State for Defence Personnel, Welfare and Veterans, Mark Francois, Commander Operations Rear Admiral Matthew Par, the United Kingdom High Commissioner in Cyprus, Matthew Kidd, and his military counterpart, Major General Richard Cripwell. A VIP visit in which I, as force commander, of course took part.

During conversations with the participants from the military, I detected some frustration that *Diamond* was not allowed into Syrian waters on the same terms as the Danish and Norwegian warships. In connection with my briefing of the delegation, I thus sensed a wish to change this state of affairs. I was asked about my view on the matter. I replied that, from a tactical perspective, I would prefer if all units in the force could enter Syrian territorial waters, but if I put on my strategic lenses, I would very much advise the British Government against pursuing the matter further. I felt that such a change would be met with fierce resistance from Russia and Syria, and that it might, at worst, put a stop to the entire operation. The Moscow Plan did not account for a British warship inside Syrian waters, and I was certain that the Russians would not accept such a change. I am not sure everyone around the table found my reply particularly helpful, but when you ask a question, you must be ready to accept the answer you are given, and that was my view on the matter. Later that day I got a chance to expand on my view with some of the British guests, and it was my impression that I had managed to shelve the matter.

That evening we were informed that the next shipment would be ready for pickup the following morning. We knew that the town and surrounding area had seen fighting since the time of the last pickup, but we did not consider a call into port any more dangerous than it had been all along.

I had decided that this time I would enter the port on board *Ark Futura*. I wanted to show the crew on the cargo ships and our personnel inside the port that I considered this safe. Uncertainty about the security after the firing incident could generate fear among those who had to call into port, and it was important for me to demonstrate my active participation alongside those members of the crew – not from a safe distance in a combat information centre at sea. In addition, I hoped to meet some of the Syrian military personnel with whom we were cooperating and possibly establish a personal rapport to help ease events going forward for everyone involved.

A Norwegian Coastal Ranger surveilling the port of Latakia from Taiko. *In the foreground is one of the port's small tugboats, which we kept an extra eye on. (L.M. Hovtun/Forsvaret.no)*

14 March

Today was pickup day, both for *Taiko* and *Ark Futura*. We were informed yesterday, and as usual we emailed the Chinese, called the Russians and made the necessary arrangements.

There is nothing to suggest that the recent attacks on Latakia are directed at the chemical transports. Instead, they have targeted the headquarters in Latakia or simply the city itself since it is home to many Alevites and other al-Assad supporters and therefore considered a perfectly legitimate target by some of the rebels. My presence in the port will show the Syrians that we still trust them to provide the necessary security, which I consider important. Last, but not least it will demonstrate to the Danish and Norwegian personnel on the cargo ships and the few members of staff inside the port that I also dare to enter it.

I was transferred to *Ark Futura* and briefed by the Chief of the Military Police, who will act as my bodyguard while I am in Syria. He told me how to behave and move in relation to the people I will be speaking to and who will be keeping an eye on me: marksmen on board the ships and frogmen at the jetty. It sounds extreme, but everyone was calm, and personally, I did not think the large array of security personnel was necessary, but it was not up for discussion.

We arrived in Latakia, where the skipper of *Ark Futura* performed the most amazing manoeuvre. He almost threw the 200-metre-long ship into port, but the last couple of metres were completely quiet, so you did not feel the actual arrival. Impressive.

Once inside the port, we had to move the scanner and all the other gear into place, and the patrol leader went to the VIP tent from which the posh senior Syrian officers observed the day's manoeuvre. He returned with an invitation to join them.

It was a surreal experience to walk across the ramp and ashore in Syria. That probably will not happen again anytime soon. I went to the tent where the atmosphere was a bit tense, though with the exception of the Syrian colonel with whom I had worked on the Moscow Plan in Russia. He was still very kind and smiling. He and I immediately began to talk, and that helped lighten the mood. Present in the tent were also the Syrian Army Chief's Deputy Commander, a high-ranking Syrian naval officer, the head of security in Latakia and in the port of Latakia and several others who did not attract much attention, though.

The VIP tent in the port of Latakia.

The conversation actually went really well. I told him that I thought the operation was going well, even though it was difficult logistically to get lorries and ships to meet in a port. We also exchanged generalities about our two countries, and the colonel commented that I looked more relaxed now than I did in Moscow. I replied that our current situation was also very different from the one in Moscow. It was actually as pleasant as a meeting like that can be. Not pleasant in the Danish sense of the word, but at least they were not hostile.

A while later a couple of Russians joined us. All the Syrians stood up and gathered around them. I was left with the colonel and my language officer, and I sensed that it was probably time to take a walk around the port, and so we left the tent. We inspected the area where the containers were stripped of the famous armour plating and repackaged. We went to the Joint Mission/OPCW building, and the soldiers there were the only ones wearing bullet-proof vests and helmets. It may be a UN or OPCW requirement, but it seemed excessive and the wrong signal to send to the Syrians. If the Syrians do not have to wear vests and helmets, neither do I. That demonstrates respect.

After talking to the UN team leader, I headed back towards the ship, still with the colonel on my left side and a bodyguard on my right. I had been given strict instructions to keep the person I would be talking to on my left side, making it easy for the bodyguard to quickly grab me if necessary.

I also got to see the scanner in action, which was very interesting. Transporting a scanner to Cyprus on a plane in December was not cheap, but it was money well spent. It could take clear pictures with colour contrasts of the material in question.

When I returned to *Ark Futura*, the Frogman Corps' boatman was waiting for me on deck and asked me if I wanted to join them in the fast dinghy. I was happy to. While we were in the harbour basin waiting, the three frogmen came up with a name for me. You see, they all have slightly odd names (KU, Hobbes, the Goat, Casanova and so on). They asked me if I wanted to be called Topper, and yes, that was fine by me. So that it is now my name when I am alone with them. They are really great guys with whom I actually enjoy spending time. They are completely straightforward and really well-balanced.

It was a great day, where I really think we came a long way with regard to establishing the good relations we so very much depend on.

Back in the waters off Cyprus we received a distinguished guest on 15 March: Chief of the Naval Command, Rear Admiral Frank Trojahn. He was picked up at 10:00, and all day his nose was kept to the grindstone with briefings and conversations and visits to *Ark Futura* and *Taiko*. It was a long day with great visits, where I for once could remain in the background and let Frank Trojahn be the centre of attention.

Frank Trojahn stayed for two days, and the second day included a visit on board the *Diamond*. While we were briefed in the destroyer's CIC, I received a message from its operations officer, who told me that my staff on *Esbern Snare* wanted to speak to me. Via the ship's encrypted channel, the staff officer on watch told me that they had just received a signal informing us that we would be picking up a shipment with *Taiko* the next day.

Frank Trojahn being welcomed on board Esbern Snare. *To the right is my Norwegian Deputy Commander, Commander Svein Erik Kvalvaag. To the left is the commander of* Esbern Snare, *Commander Senior Grade Søren Thinggaard Larsen.*

I immediately ordered *Diamond* to move to the waters off Latakia and start putting together a situational picture of the area. While the Brits prepared to get underway, my operations officer on *Esbern Snare* and I put together a plan that he and the rest of the staff could then translate into an order for the force. We decided that *Esbern Snare* would remain outside Cyprus, and that Frank Trojahn and I would go ashore in Larnaca that evening, as the plan was for me to return home on leave together with the rear admiral.

In the meantime, *Diamond* would move to the holding area, where *Ark Futura* and *Taiko* were waiting, and put together a situational overview the area. Finally, the Norwegian frigate in Limassol was ordered to put out to sea in time for it to arrive outside Latakia at 11:00 on 17 March.

Concurrently with the planning, I received a message from Per Moll, our liaison officer at the OPCW mission headquarters in Cyprus, saying that Sigrid Kaag wanted to speak to me. She would have to wait, though, until we had planned all aspects of the pickup, and I did not manage to get back to her until 17:30. During our conversation, I once again took the opportunity to call for an overall – and realistic – plan for the remaining pickups. I argued that without such a plan we risked finding ourselves in a situation where we would be unable to perform a pickup. In reply, Sigrid simply said that she considered such a situation unthinkable. I thought about that for a while; after all, it was only unthinkable if we accepted a situation where we scraped through without knowing what would happen the next day. Apparently, the OPCW did not appreciate what was required to coordinate the movements, crew rotation, logistics, etc. of a naval force.

Of course, Sigrid Kaag's assessment was based on the belief that getting the Syrians to draw up a useable plan for us was not realistic, and she was probably right, and we just had to deal with that. We therefore chose to turn the process upside down and draw up a plan that suited us and which the OPCW could then use in their ongoing negotiations with the Syrians. Yet this solution was problematic, as it enabled the Syrians to use the plan to bother us. For example, they could choose to deliver chemical substances to Latakia on days when it did not suit us to collect them, because we had planned a supply visit to Limassol that day, for example. Our plan therefore had to be flexible, so it did not catch us off guard.

After talking to Sigrid Kaag, I left for the airport and Denmark. I had neither had time to pack nor prepare anything for my return journey, so I was suddenly in a hurry. Fortunately, Frank Trojahn and I managed to arrive in time.

***

I returned to *Esbern Snare* on the evening of 26 March after the best leave imaginable.

I had followed the situation from home and knew that while I had been away, the pickups had stopped once again. But this time al-Assad's forces could not be blamed for the delay. Instead the security situation in Latakia had worsened significantly for the forces loyal to al-Assad. Since the rocket attacks on 9 March, the rebel forces had managed to take ground around the city. And the opposition targeted supporters of President al-Assad, of whom there were quite a lot in Latakia. The city therefore constituted a major military target for the rebels who were enjoying battlefield gains those days.

Since 9 March, the frequency of rocket attacks had increased, and they basically hit all parts of the city. The opposition had publicly announced that they were targeting the governmental buildings and other infrastructure in the city supporting al-Assad's grip on Latakia, but of course (as we had learned) the problems was that the rockets did not always hit their intended targets.

All of this had increased the risk of one of our lorries carrying chemical substances being hit on their way to the port or that a stray rocket might hit one of the ships. Under these circumstances, all we could do was to wait for the regime to regain control of Latakia and its environs, eliminating the rebel forces' ability to hit the port. In mid-March al-Assad's forces had launched a military campaign to do just that, but they still had not managed to gain full control over the city and its environs.

While we waited for the situation in Latakia to change, we continued our training. On 27 March, for example, we conducted a large-scale sea rescue exercise together with the Cypriot sea rescue authorities and the Cypriot police. Among other things, the exercise included evacuation of personnel from the ships by three Cypriot helicopters. The exercise was a success and highly relevant, as *Esbern Snare*'s helicopter would be flying to Cyprus the following day to be transported back home for service by one of the Royal Danish Air Force's transport aircraft – and it was not going to be replaced by another helicopter, mind you. This reduced our evacuation potential by 50 per cent, as the British *Diamond* was now the only ship with access to a helicopter. Training with others was therefore important, as it would ease our cooperation in case we needed to transfer wounded personnel to a hospital in Cyprus fast.

March 27 was also the day when Svein Erik Kvalvaag left the force to return to Norway. His replacement, Captain Bjørn-Erik Marthinsen, joined us the following week.

While I was on leave, people back home had decided that due to the fighting around Latakia, it would be a good idea for the ships to move further out to sea to reduce the risk of an attack. The Deputy Commander, who had acted as force commander while I was away, had done as requested. I did not agree with the plan, though, as I still considered it important to show our presence and ability to pick up shipments at short notice. I therefore moved the force back to the holding area where it had been waiting before I went home on leave. By doing so, I hoped our presence would put pressure on the Syrians to get the shipments of chemical substances going again. We had been told that al-Assad's forces – supervised by the OPCW – were packing containers incessantly throughout the country, and we took that as a sign that they would begin to transport containers to Latakia as soon as the security situation permitted.

Of course waiting in the holding area was a bit riskier, seeing as the fighting was taking place close by, but there was still no indication that we constituted a target. I therefore felt that moving the ships closer to the coast was a responsible move, and the following day *Esbern Snare* had returned to the area outside Latakia. From here we could follow the fighting on shore, and that evening we witnessed a large number of detonations north of the city and a barrage of machine gun fire. It was difficult to say how close they were to the city centre, but there was no doubt that the fighting was thick.

Esbern Snare patrolled the area until 28 March, where we returned to Limassol to receive another VIP guest the following day, namely the US Under Secretary of State for Arms Control and International Security, Rose Gottemoeller.

At 09:00 on 29 March, Rose Gottemoeller and her personal assistant arrived on *Diamond*'s helicopter along with the Danish and Norwegian ambassadors in Cyprus. We gave them a warm welcome, before they were guided into the officer's mess for coffee, homemade Danish pastries and fruit. Here I held a very informal briefing about the operation. Rose Gottemoeller asked a lot of questions and was particularly interested in our relationship with the Russians and the Russian/Chinese cooperation.

I informed her in detail about the operation and the entire lead-up with the meeting in Moscow in December, synchronisation of our plan and the Russian one, as well as the result hereof. We then detailed the pickups and showed Rose Gottemoeller a lot of pictures from Latakia, including ones of the rocket attacks we had experienced. With regard to the Russians, I told her that we did not have any problems at my level. They had visited us three times, and each time we had parted as good friends and colleagues. I did tell Rose Gottemoeller directly that I did not really need the Russian and Chinese units to complete the task, though, and that I would actually prefer to have them at arm's length. I was unfamiliar with their Rules of Engagement and therefore did not know how they would react in the event of threats against us. It was an element of insecurity that we would rather be without.

Similarly, I informed her that of course I understood the need to cooperate with the Russians for strategic reasons and that I fully accepted that the Russians acted as the coordinating party, because the important thing was to keep the operation going. And after all, I knew who really commanded the ships in my fleet. This was where the cargo ships belonged, and they did not call into port before I ordered them to, no matter how much the Russians wanted to be called the coordinating party.

I also told Rose Gottemoeller that we – due to our liaison officer in the OPCW mission headquarters in Cyprus – always received information about the transports before the Russians, and that we had been the ones to call them each time to inform them of future pickups and how we intended to collect the chemical substances.

The briefing was followed by the obligatory tour of the ship, where our Finnish specialists once again expertly demonstrated how they would clean individuals contaminated by chemical substances.

All things considered, it was a successful visit by someone who was not unimportant. As number three in the US Department of State, Rose

Rose Gottemoeller receives the Esbern Snare *coat of arms as a memento of her visit.*

Gottemoeller wielded great influence. She also spoke very honestly about conversations she had had with the US Secretary of State, John Kerry, and the Russian Minister of Foreign Affairs, Sergey Lavrov, in this strange situation, to put it mildly, where both nations supported Operation RECSYR, but disagreed completely about other issues, including the developments in the Crimea.

30 March
The wind has picked up speed, reaching 18-20 m/s, and the waves have risen to a height 5-6 metres. This does not really affect a 6,500-ton ship, but it is enough to make the crew quiet. The majority of the crew is not used to high waves after many years of fighting piracy in the Indian Ocean, which rarely sees waves of this size. But I enjoyed feeling the sea and being on a ship. They are still fighting north of Latakia, but there are beginning indications that al-Assad's forces are getting things under control. That is good news for us. But of course it is a very odd operation and situation, where I, contrary to all other contexts, have to work closely together with the Russians, and where it is good news for me and the operation if al-Assad's forces manage to defeat the rebel forces and gain ground around Latakia. A bit bizarre.

The next couple of days *Esbern Snare* will undergo crew rotation. The crew that started the operation last December after having spent three months in the Indian Ocean were relieved by the *Absalon* crew on 15 January. At the time, they had been at sea for four months. They are now returning after two and a half months at home and will be with us for the next six weeks, before they will be replaced by the frigate *Peter Willemoes.*

Once again it was time for crew rotation on *Esbern Snare*, so while *Diamond* kept watch over *Ark Futura* and *Taiko* just outside Cypriot territorial waters, the support ship and *Helge Ingstad* docked in Limassol on 31 March.

The crew spent the next two days packing, and on 2 April we said goodbye to around 120 crew members who would be replaced by a similar number arriving from Denmark that afternoon.

The 'new' crew was the one who had started the mission, and whom I had said goodbye to back in January. They had spent the past two and a half months at home, and another deployment this soon was in fact a bit over the top. Our contribution to Operation RECSYR pushed the Danish Navy, and the Second Squadron in particular, to the limit, and this naturally affected both the deployed personnel and their families back home.

I gave a speech to the crew about to return home, thanking them for their good work, both as a flag ship and as Denmark's contribution to Operation RECSYR. I also told them that I shared their frustration with the tempo of the operation. However, this did not change the fact that we had so far picked up around 50 per cent of the chemical substances, and that was after all that mattered and what I urged them to focus on. The photo shows the crew in Limassol on 19 May 2014.

It was my impression, though, that the new crew was motivated all the same, because the job still made a lot of sense. The new crew was the one that had started things and who had participated in the first pickup on 7 January 2014. They also very much wanted to be the ones to complete the last one. This was not unrealistic, if only the Syrians rebels would stop firing rockets in Latakia.

The change of crew made me consider asking Frank Trojahn for a replacement for myself. I still could not believe I had been given the chance to lead an operation of this kind, and from a professional point of view, I never thought I would experience anything greater. However, this did not change the fact that I missed my family immensely and *truly* wanted to return home to them.

I felt torn because professionally I wanted to finish the job. It made really good sense for me to continue as commander because of the many important personal relations I had established, not least with the Russians and Syrians. These relations had already proved valuable on several occasions, and it would take time for a new commander to build equally good relations – not least considering the current situation concerning the Crimea and Ukraine.

On the other hand, I could feel that the absence of my family had begun to affect my personal motivation.

There was no room for indecision since if my men got the impression that I no longer believed in the cause, it would spread like wildfire. After careful deliberation, I decided not to ask for a replacement, at least for the time being. This was due both to the above-mentioned deliberations, and that the new crew seemed very motivated and ready for the operation and were proud to be allowed to remove chemical substances from Syria. I did not wish to undermine their pride in serving.

At the end of March, it seemed like the Syrian regime had regained control of the area around Latakia. According to our intelligence, the al-Assad forces had deployed up to 5,000 soldiers and conducted severe air raids to restore calm. We therefore expected to be able to call into port safely soon, even though the Syrians refused to guarantee that we would not see any more rocket attacks.

It was really an odd situation: To be able to pick up the chemical weapons, we needed the Syrian Government to suppress the rebel forces that we would call freedom fighters as soon as the operation was over.

We still had no official date for the next pickup, but we heard of high-level discussions about a forthcoming recommencement. And as soon as that happened, we could expect the shipments to arrive one after the other. In order to be ready, *Esbern Snare* left Limassol on 3 April, and the crew set about doing various training exercises. This included hailing via the ship's loudspeakers at a frequency that almost made me go mad. Another example of the fact that my fuse was getting shorter. It was hard for me not to be irritated, especially considering the lack of news regarding future pickups.

The Norwegian frigate in Limassol.

Finally, we received the long-awaited news of a pickup on 4 April, and we did the routine calls and preparations, which included drawing up the specific order for the ships regarding the pickup.

The plan had been for the Norwegian frigate, also in Limassol, to follow us out to sea, but it was delayed. It was 22:00 before *Helge Ingstad* was ready to leave the port, and at that hour no pilot or tugboats were available to help the frigate navigate out of the port. The Norwegians therefore informed my officer on watch that they were forced to wait for the pilot and tugboats to arrive at 06:00 the following morning. This meant that they would not be ready outside Latakia at 08:00 as planned. This was unacceptable to me. It was still vital for us to follow the Moscow Plan to the letter, and I therefore had to call the commander of the Norwegian frigate to explain to him that if he was not in place outside Latakia the next morning, the Russians might use this as a pretext for sending one of their warships into our area to replace *Helge Ingstad*. He promised me that they would put out to sea during the night, in time for them to reach the waters off Latakia the following morning. And he kept his word, because when the sun rose *Helge Ingstad* was on station and ready.

4 April

We arrived in the area at 08:00, just in time for transferring the liaison officers at 08:30. The pickup was a success. We picked up eight containers. The city was calm, but there was some activity in the air north of Latakia, where Syrian fighters and helicopters were attacking the opposition.

The new crew did well, even though they of course do things a bit differently compared to the former crew. This pickup was probably the one with the best timing. Everything fit like a glove. It took 72 minutes from the moment they set to work on the jetty till they closed the ramps on *Ark Futura* again. In total, the operation took six hours with land and sea transport, and it involved nine ships (five from my force, two from the Russian/Chinese and two Syrian torpedo/missile vessels) and up to 2,000 soldiers in Syria. Logistically, it is a complex process – even though picking up eight containers in a port sounds simple enough.

Syrian lorries loaded with chemical substances arrive in a part of the port that has been enclosed by two layers of containers to protect the area from rocket fragments in the event of an attack.

Relieved

Despite my previous deliberations, I decided on 4 April to ask Frank Trojahn to be relieved as commander of the operation. I recommended the replacement take place at a later date, which would allow time for my Norwegian Deputy Commander to become acquainted with the job, enabling him to run the operation until a new Danish commander, appointed by the Naval Command back home, would arrive.

I had changed my mind regarding replacement due to the continued lack of a date for the completion of the mission. This uncertainty was really eating into me. I spent too much time thinking about it, and it made me miss my family back home even more, and I therefore could not see myself complete the operation. I really wanted to have been able to complete the mission, which would also have made the most sense considering the personal relations I had established with the commander of *Pyotr Velikiy*, the Chinese, the Syrians and the OPCW. But there is an end to everything, and I had come to that end, so I wrote to Frank Trojahn asking to be relieved. And having made the decision, I actually felt relieved.

Even though I had made the decision to be relieved, the operation continued, and we had now come to a point where we had to involve the Americans on transferring the first-priority substances to *Cape Ray*, which was waiting at the Spanish naval base of Rota. On 5 April I launched this part of the operation by sending an email to the Americans – the commander of the US Navy's operations in the Mediterranean, the Deputy Commander in the US Europe Command and the Deputy Commander in the US Defence Threat Reduction Agency in Washington, respectively.

On 6 April my new Norwegian Deputy Commander, Captain Bjørn-Erik Marthinsen, joined us. The plan had originally been for him to arrive 10 days earlier, but he had had to stay in Norway for family reasons. I had had to make do without a Deputy Commander and was looking forward to a well-deserved break from some of my day-to-day tasks. We talked for a long time that evening, and I got a good impression of the 50-year-old captain. He was extremely motivated, and I was certain that we would have a good working relationship. Bjørn-Erik did not seem afraid to set to work, and that felt good, because it enabled me to step back from time to time when I felt like it.

Seeing as the Syrians still had not provided us with a plan for the remaining pickups, we tried to ease our planning by using the first 12 pickups to draw up a list of the days they had taken place. We thus hoped to be able to predict upcoming pickups. Statistically, it was a rather fragile foundation, but we felt it was worth the try.

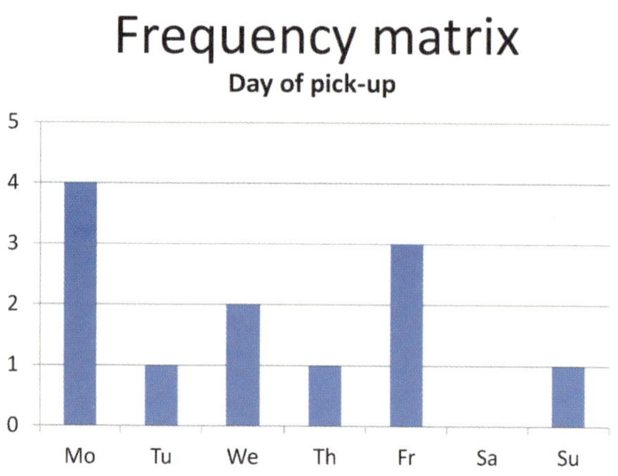

Comparison between week-day and week-end.
Conclusion: The Syrians tend to 92% NOT to use the week-end. They tend to postpone until Monday and be done by Friday.

Our statistics suggested that we could expect a new shipment to arrive in Latakia the following Monday; unfortunately, this did not transpire. That Sunday we were informed that Latakia had suffered two rocket attacks the previous day, and on Sunday night we received news of more rocket attacks on the city. The Syrians therefore informed us that we once again had to await an evaluation of the security situation before new transports would be initiated.

This was frustrating because all we could do was wait. The rocket threat had been there all along, and if the Syrians wanted to wait for it to be eliminated completely, we might have to wait for a long time for the next shipment.

We therefore began to plan for the eventuality that we had to sail to Italy with the 80 containers of chemical substances already on board *Taiko* and *Ark Futura* and then back to Latakia, hopefully to pick up the remaining containers. After all, it made no sense to wait for weeks off the coast of Syria if there was no real chance of more shipments arriving anytime soon. We had to go about things quietly, though, because if the Syrians found out about these plans, we feared that it would make them lose all motivation to recommence pickups.

Concurrently with our attempt using statistics to calculate possible dates for future pickups, we also conducted what in military terms is called Situational Awareness or SA for short. This involved observing the Syrians' behaviour before and during pickups. Based on previous pickups, we could tell that the Syrians generally emptied the port of civilian ships the evening before a pickup. And the first week of April we watched cargo ships enter and exit the port of Latakia, which we took to be a sign that the security situation was not as poor as the Syrians claimed, and that they did not plan to do any pickups in the near future. At the same time, we received a signal that Sigrid Kaag would be attending a meeting in Latakia the following Wednesday, and we therefore did not expect chemical substances to arrive that day either.

A container on board Taiko *being inspected by Norwegian specialists in full protective gear. (S. Rudi/forsvaret.no)*

On 9 April we were informed that two of the containers on board *Taiko* were 'sweating'. When the sun was up, the temperature inside the containers rose, and so did the pressure in the chemical substances inside the container. The containers in question contained second-priority material, that is, the less dangerous types of substances. Nevertheless, the Norwegians had chosen to contact the OPCW in The Hague because they did not know what to do. This constituted a clear breach of our procedures for such events, which we had been practising over and over again these past months. Sitting in The Hague, all the OPCW could do was worry and therefore send well-meaning but distracting emails to us about the matter. The Americans also learned of the incident, and our liaison officer in Cyprus, Per Moll, had to work hard that day to keep everyone calm.

Due to the incident, I had to impress on the top military command on board *Taiko* that the chain of command went through me. I could and would not accept that they went behind my back and contacted the OPCW directly – even if it was with the best of intentions. Disturbance in the chain of command causes disturbance in the organisation as a whole. The Norwegians promised me that it would not happen again, but unfortunately did the exact same thing in a later report. I therefore had to ask my Norwegian Deputy Commander to impress – in unmistakable terms – on his fellow countrymen that they had to observe the chain of command.

10 April

It was pickup day for *Ark Futura*. Everything went by the book, until one of the containers showed too high a level of contamination.

Just like when the rockets had hit Latakia while we were inside the port, I thought I sensed too much insecurity on the communication networks.

In the port, everything was quiet, no rockets or anything, so we actually had time to think. Nevertheless, the Frogman Crops' dinghy was ordered to leave the port immediately to go pick up some of the chemical specialists on board *Esbern Snare*. On the staff room camera, I watched the dinghy race – as ordered – out of the port at 40 plus knots. They had to get specialists on board *Ark Futura* to inspect the containers.

This was all very well, but let us assess the situation together with the chemical specialists already present first. I had to step in and veto the decision in order to stop it and make people stop to think instead of just going off on a tangent.

We need to hurry slowly, think carefully and do the right thing. No one had informed the Russians of what we intended to do, even though this is very important, as it might otherwise cause them to worry. The Syrians had no idea that we had sent dinghies at high speed out to *Esbern Snare*. They were patrolling the area just outside the port in their own dinghies, and if they suddenly saw a dinghy sail right towards them at high speed, they might open fire. Such a decision must be coordinated with and communicated to everyone, including the Russians. Just as we agreed in Moscow, and just as I have said over and over again.

A Syrian armoured fighting vehicle escorting the lorries to Latakia.

I wanted to discuss this with my own chemical advisers first, before we began doing all kind of things. We use two different forms of signalling when we choose to deploy specialists. Some may believe that it is because we do not trust the OPCW specialists, but instead it shows our personnel and *Ark Futura* that we have things under control and are able to handle situations like this one. After some discussion and briefing of my own specialists, I decided to send specialists into the port in full gear, regardless of whether some might take it to mean that we do not fully trust the Syrians and the OPCW (which are the ones responsible for security).

This time we did not have to hurry to inform the Russians and Syrians in the port.

The inspection took some time, as the container had to be repackaged, supplied with new litter and aired. The new measurement showed the same result: The figures were too high.

According to the information I received over the radio, there were clear signs of spillage from the drum, and the valves were rusty. We decided there and then that we would not allow this container on board *Ark Futura* until it had been repackaged and cleaned. This was the first time we had turned a container away!

‘Norwegian Syria Soldiers in Bomb Drama!’

As previously mentioned, our approach to the press was generally very positive, and we had been as open towards them as is possible during a military operation like this one. In my opinion, this had paid off in the form of a series of positive articles and TV segments, which had helped tell our story to the rest of the world. However, there is no such thing as a thorn-less rose, and on 11 April the Norwegian newspaper VG ran an article titled ‘Norwegian Syria Soldiers in Bomb Drama!’ In dramatic terms, the article related the story of the episode on 9 March, where Latakia had been hit by rockets while we were collecting a shipment of chemical substances. The article suggested that the rockets were meant for the Danish and Norwegian ships, which of course was not pleasant to read for our loved ones back home. Especially considering that we had chosen not to make the story public. Apparently, the commander of *Helge Ingstad* was the source of the story, which appeared far more dramatic than we at *Esbern Snare* remembered it. That is not surprising, though, seeing as the objective was to attract readers. Several aspects of the story were incorrect, and overall it presented the operation as extremely dangerous. I asked the commander of *Helge Ingstad* to explain, and shortly afterwards I received an explanation and an apology from the commander, who regretted having told the reporter about the incident.

To me, the article confirmed that our proactive suggestion on 9 March to make the incident public – in order to deflate it – had been the right thing to do. I immediately informed the Naval Command in Aarhus and attached a copy of the article, informing them that there was a risk that the Danish media might also pick up the story. I therefore urged the Naval Command to draw up a response and proactively issue a press statement or similar on the matter. Once again, to my frustration, they chose not to comment on the Norwegian article and instead passively await further activity.

Helge Ingstad *and* Esbern Snare *performing Replenishment at Sea from the French supply ship* Var *on 12 April 2014. The three ships are sailing at a speed of approx. 10 knots and at a distance of approx. 30 metres. The American supply ship had left the area back in March, and we were therefore pleased that the French Navy enabled us to refuel with the help of* Var, *which meant that we did not have to call at port in Limassol.*

The article was problematic for two reasons: Loved ones back home might worry unnecessarily, as the article described Operation RECSYR as being more dangerous than it really was. At the same time, the Syrians might once again use the publicity to delay the pickups, arguing that it was too dangerous for *Taiko* and *Ark Futura* to call into Latakia. Fortunately, the Syrians never took advantage of the situation, and the case died down.

13 April

Once again it was pickup day, and tactically and procedure-wise it has very much become routine. I issued directives during the morning meeting, the main message being that we must hurry slowly in case of unforeseen events. Let us use the specialists already available to us and find the best solution instead of rushing without thought into a quick decision. If time and circumstances are on our side, we should take the time to do our best.

We are once again planning a visit from the Danish Minister of Defence. He wants to revisit us and join us on the last pickup. The problem is just that we do not know when the last pickup will be. We do not know until we are heading into Latakia. We can suspect – when there are e.g. eight containers left – that the next pickup will be the last, but of course we cannot know for sure. They can choose to arrive with just three, or we may have to reject one or more containers, and then suddenly it was not the last pickup after all. Sometimes it is difficult for me to understand how little sense of the operation they have or wish to have back home.

I can understand the communicative and strategic needs, sure, but not how these things can pass through the entire bureaucratic management chain without anything of real professional value being added. We have actually made an effort to tell them back home about the logistic challenges we face down here, and this is difficult to plan – and you should not have to be out here to understand that. Well, that is me letting off steam!

On 14 April, we paid a quick visit to Limassol to stock up on supplies. We had to get supplies for the rest of the operation and *Esbern Snare*'s next mission in the Indian Ocean.

Also in the port was the French destroyer *Dupleix*, which had invited me over for lunch a couple of weeks previously. I now had a chance to return the gesture and invite the French commander and his operations officer for lunch on *Esbern Snare*. The French supported us with tanker capacity, among other things, and it was important to maintain good relations with them. This turned out to be useful a couple of days later when we needed to get one of the officers on *Esbern Snare* to a hospital in Cyprus. As mentioned, the support ship's helicopter had returned to Denmark, so we had to ask *Dupleix* politely whether they would make their helicopter available to us, which eased the transfer of the sick officer significantly. The following day they even went into Cyprus to pick up the officer and return him to *Esbern Snare*.

After an enjoyable lunch we spent the rest of the day planning the phase of the operation that would begin once we have got the last chemical substances on board and had to escort *Ark Futura* and *Taiko* to various places in Europe for the destruction of their cargo.

At this point we had collected more than 80 per cent of the chemical substances, and it was extremely frustrating to learn that 46 containers were ready and waiting in the Syrian city of Homs. Al-Assad's forces refused to take them to Latakia, as they did not consider it safe enough. To us, it looked like another Syrian stalling attempt, but once again there was nothing we could do.

16 April

It was pickup day again. It looks like an invasion force out here immediately before pickups and when we call at port: four warships and a couple of cargo ships sailing at a decent clip towards the port.

Ark Futura, Helge Ingstad, Pyotr Velikiy *and* Taiko *off the coast of Syria.*

When we were a couple of nautical miles from the port, we suddenly saw five or six plumes of smoke around the city. It had emerged suddenly, initially black, then turning white. It was difficult to see what had caused it. Understandably, *Esbern Snare* reported it as possible rocket attacks, but otherwise the city looked calm. Traffic was flowing and people were moving about as usual. So we had to act fast to determine the cause. I asked *Ark Futura* to ask the pilot if he knew what it was. He said that it was normal 'Latakia smoke'. At the same time, the staff looked into it via open sources (e.g. Twitter), because if it was rockets, it would soon be mentioned here, and our liaison officer in Cyprus called Latakia for news about the situation. According to all available sources, everything was calm, and on that basis we decided to continue into port.

This time we had miscalculated the land transport, because we arrived an hour before the first lorry. Otherwise everything went according to plan, and none of the containers with the nerve gas component showed spillage. We had previously reported these incidents as 'leakages', but that had caused difficulties in the US, which believe the incidents should be referred to as 'spillage' or 'spills'. Well, it is not our first language, so let us call it 'spillage' if that is what it takes to calm people down. The challenge is the same to us, no matter what you call it.

This time we did not have problems with the containers, but the scanner overheated, and it would take half an hour to scan the last container. I was asked if we should leave it, but as everything seemed peaceful I decided to stay and wait for it.

That evening I watched a film in the officers' mess with the doctor and my chief of staff. Even though I fell asleep halfway through the film, it was a good ending to another pickup.

The next day I called all the commanders to a meeting on *Esbern Snare*, but the commander of *Ark Futura* had to cancel, as he had to stay on the ship to monitor the opening of one of the containers holding nerve gas components.

A reading of the container had shown a change, and it was therefore necessary to open it to identify the cause. It was cleaned, and the reading was repeated. Everything was good.

When I contacted our liaison officer in Cyprus later that afternoon to see if there was any news, he told me that there was not because the OPCW mission headquarters had been closed for Easter. The OPCW's role was simply to support and facilitate the mission, and we had been told over and over again that the participating nations were responsible for solving the task, but we nevertheless felt that the OPCW could have shown us the respect of at least keeping their office in Cyprus open with a minimum of staff despite the holiday.

On the evening of 18 April, we were once again told at short notice that we would be picking up 16 containers the following day containing the main components for the nerve gasses sarin and VX. As previously we tried to pass the information on to the Russians but were unable to contact *Pyotr Velikiy* in Limassol. We knew that the cruiser was set to return to Russia soon and had learned from the Russian defence attaché in Cyprus that it would be replaced by the flagship of the Russian Black Sea Fleet, the cruiser *Moskva*. However, as it had not arrived in the waters off Cyprus yet, it seemed like the job would go to the Russian destroyer *Admiral Levchenko*. And when we called the Russian defence attaché, he gave us the number for *Admiral Levchenko*. We then called the destroyer to agree on a time and place to meet the following morning. During the conversation it became clear that the staff on board the destroyer had no knowledge of procedures and had not been briefed about the content of the Moscow Plan.

I therefore arranged for my liaison officer to take the plan together with the code word and other information to *Admiral Levchenko* and on that basis 'talk the Russians through' the pickup. This had to be done with diplomatic ingenuity, because the last thing we wanted was to humiliate the Russians, and on the surface at least, it had to appear as though the Russians were on top of things.

19 April

We met with *Admiral Levchenko* as agreed and exchanged liaison officers. This time we received two well-groomed, young and very friendly Russian naval officers, one of whom spoke English very well. He had lived in Scotland for a year. At the same time, our military linguist went over to *Admiral Levchenko* carrying the Moscow Plan. He will be able to explain everything.

It suddenly hit us: Where are the Chinese? Here we were about to call at port, and our Chinese friend was not here. He was in the middle of the sea between Cyprus and Syria. There was no doubt that the Russians once again had not informed the Chinese that today was pickup day. We immediately sent our Chinese colleague an email and received a quick reply: 'DAMN!'

I also contacted Per Moll in Cyprus who would get in touch with the Chinese and Russian liaison officers to make sure the Chinese received the information via the right channels – that is, from the Russians. It is a Russian/Chinese fleet, and I still remember the preliminary phases of the mission and must be careful not to be considered the overall commander of the mission; I do not wish to humiliate anyone.

The pickup went according to plan. This time we got a reading on three of the containers. We had two of them cleaned, but liquid DF (the main component for the nerve gas sarin) was leaking from the third container and through the paint, which was bubbling, so we left it in Latakia.

On 22 April we picked up another 15 containers. Now only nine containers from the area around the city of Homs and 16 from the Damascus area were left. We were very unsure when the latter would arrive, as the OPCW so far did not have access to them because the area was seeing heavy fighting. Nevertheless, the OPCW was very optimistic and continued telling us that they expected them to be ready for pickup sometime soon.

On 20 April the chaplain performed a well-attended Easter service in the cafeteria on Esbern Snare. *I spent the rest of the day and the following one tending to various administrative tasks while waiting for news from the OPCW.*

Our message to the ships was therefore that we expected another pickup within the next 48 to 72 hours – even though I personally had my doubts as to whether this was realistic.

On 23 April it was election day for the European Parliament and the Unified Patent Court. At sea such an election is conducted more or less the same way as on land with appointed officers and is a good experience, often with a high turnout.

Last, but not least it was the Chinese fleet's birthday, and I took the opportunity to congratulate the commander of the Chinese frigate and thank them for their assistance during Operation RECSYR. Shortly afterwards we received a nice thank you signal in return.

My Last Pickup

On 24 April we called at port together with *Ark Futura* to pick up the last nine containers from the area around Homs. I once again joined them and was assigned a bodyguard who once again went over my movements and reactions in case of unsuspected events. I still felt that a personal bodyguard was a bit over the top, but I also realised that in an Arabic country having a bodyguard is a status symbol. For that reason only, it might be worth it. This time I had brought a couple of coats of arms, some good-looking framed photographs of *Esbern Snare* and a stack of T-shirts with the ship's logo to present to the staff in Latakia as presents.

When we docked, the Syrian colonel, Sareem, whom I had met in Moscow back in December 2013, was ready to greet me by the ramp. He then followed me to the VIP area, where I met General Shariff, the fleet commander, Vice Admiral al-Haffei, and an unnamed rear admiral, whose areas of responsibility I was not informed of. A couple of minutes later the Dutch UN Diplomat Sigrid Kaag joined us.

Already on our way to the VIP area, the colonel informed me that we were now witnessing the end of Operation RECSYR. I asked him about the 16 containers from the Damascus area that still had not arrived and was told that the area was still seeing severe fighting and that the Syrians therefore were unable to go and collect them. My intelligence unit on board *Esbern Snare* had confirmed that the area suffered from daily fighting and that the Syrians were not lying to us, but that did not change the fact that my mission included picking up the last containers from the Damascus area.

Shortly afterwards General Shariff and the fleet commander repeated what Colonel Sareem had said, and like the colonel they made it clear that they considered this the last pickup in Latakia for a new long time. In that connection they asked me what we planned to do with our ships after the day's pickup. They were very surprised when I told them that we would remain off the coast of Syria, waiting for the last containers.

When Pyotr Velikiy *left the mission area for Russia on 24 April, we marked the event with a so-called 'Steam Past' where both crews line up along the railing, and we fire salutes to wish each other good luck and good speed. A couple of days earlier the Russian aircraft carrier* Admiral Kuznetsov *had also left the area, heading for Severomorsk.*

The Syrians' expectation that this was the end of the mission was supported by the OPCW staff in Latakia, who told me that as soon as we had completed the day's pickup, they would begin to pack up and move their equipment to Damascus where they would await news of the last containers from a safer location.

The fact that we had said goodbye to *Pyotr Velikiy* the same morning was another indication that we were not likely to see anymore pickups in the near future. We had previously been told that the cruiser would remain in the area until the operation had been completed.

All in all, these were clear indications that we should not expect to receive more shipments for a while, perhaps not at all – but it was also clear to me that if I had not joined the ships in Latakia on 24 April and had such a good relationship with the Syrians, we probably would not have been told that they considered the operation to be over.

Even though I had told the Syrian officers that we would wait in the waters off Syria, we knew that this might not be an option after all.

Summer was just around the corner with high Mediterranean temperatures, and we did not know how the chemical substances on board the two cargo ships would react. After all, while in Syrian custody the material had been placed in bunkers at cool temperatures, and we had already seen several of the containers on board *Taiko* 'sweat' or actually leak poisonous material in the heat. I would therefore have difficulties guaranteeing their safety, if I asked *Ark Futura* and *Taiko* to wait for the last containers for several months under the summer sun. Both ships also had to sail for weeks when relocating from the waters off Syria to the planned ports of disembarkation in Italy, Great Britain and Finland, among other places.

When I sent a signal back home with the day's news, the Naval Command sent a signal back asking us to stay in the area between Cyprus and Syria until we had more information on whether and, in that case, when we could expect the last shipment to be ready for pickup. At the same time, we had to determine whether it made sense for *Ark Futura* to transfer its first-priority substances to *Cape Ray* and unload its second-priority substances in an Italian port. The only unknown quantity in that plan was whether it was safe to let *Taiko* wait in the summer heat off Syria, or whether it too should relocate to the planned ports of disembarkation. In that case, *Ark Futura* would have to remain.

We had also been told that the 16 remaining containers included five holding first-priority substances and 11 holding second-priority substances. We therefore also had to consider how long we wanted to wait for such a – relatively – small amount of second-priority substances. This decision had to be made at levels above mine, though I could influence the decision through the various connections I had established over the last six months, and after thinking about it for 24 hours I decided, among other things, to inform my American colleagues about the situation. Several of them held high-ranking positions in the American system, and we had been in regular contact throughout the operation. I found it important to inform them directly, and I had after all given the Danish Naval Command a 24-hour 'head start'. To me it was vital that the information reached the US as soon as possible, so I took a risk, even though it was more or less at odds with the official chain of command.

My message prompted an immediate reaction from the Americans. I was subsequently told that less than two hours after my email had

The mobile scanner arriving in Latakia.

reached them, Rose Gottemoeller's office in the US State Department had contacted Sigrid Kaag for an explanation of events and what the OPCW had done to ensure that the last 16 containers would eventually be removed from Syria. I do not know exactly how Sigrid Kaag or the OPCW responded, but it was clear that the Americans were not satisfied with a solution that did not include picking up all the containers – including the ones held in the area around Damascus.

While the OPCW discussed things with the Americans, we spent 26 April at sea conducting a large logistics operation, among other things. The Finnish specialists who had so far been based on *Esbern Snare* had to be transferred to *Taiko*, as we expected the ship to sail to Finland soon to unload its chemical cargo. This involved 13 transfers of Finnish

Equipment being transferred from Esbern Snare *to* Taiko.

equipment via the support ship's dinghy. Hard work for everyone involved. At the same time, we received a visit from two chemical specialists from the US who had to determine how the chemical substances on board *Ark Futura* were packed in order to prepare for their transfer to *Cape Ray*. They did what they had come to do and left again later that day with more information on what they would be receiving soon.

27 April
As expected, the Syrians missed another pickup. My motivation for continuing this journal has disappeared, so I will end it here.

On 30 April 2014 Helge Ingstad *was replaced by the Norwegian coastguard ship* Andenes. *Here seen together with the Russian destroyer* Viceadmiral Kulakov *(in the middle) and* Helge Ingstad *(in the background) during an exercise in 2011. (forsvaret.no)*

As evident from the last journal entry from 27 April 2014, I was very frustrated to learn that we had to continue to wait for clarification concerning the last shipment. I have to admit that I spent a lot of energy building motivation personally and in the force and among my own staff. A difficult balancing act. I had now participated actively in the mission for six months – since November 2013 and so far until late April 2014 – which in itself is not extremely long, but never knowing when it would end. I really wanted to complete this historic mission, but because of uncertainty about how long it would last, I now saw no other option than to be relieved. I missed Kirsten and my boys, and regardless of my ardent wish to complete this endeavour, my first priority is my family – and how I was looking forward to seeing them again.

I remember feeling extremely relieved, but also sad to walk down *Esbern Snare*'s gangway on 15 May 2014 to go ashore in Cyprus and fly home to Denmark. Operation RECSYR had been the greatest professional challenge I had seen in my 31 years in the Royal Danish Navy, and

In connection with the replacement of Esbern Snare *with* Peter Willemoes, *the two ships sailed side by side in the waters off Limassol on 25 May. This photo of the two ships was taken from* Peter Willemoes' *Lynx helicopter, whose heavy machine gun is visible in the right-hand side of the picture.*

now I did not get to complete it. But how I was looking forward to seeing my family again!

My replacement as commander of Operation RECSYR was Captain Steen Engelbrecht Petersen, who arrived the day I left for home. At the same time, the frigate *Peter Willemoes* was on its way to the area to replace *Esbern Snare* two days later. The Danish force would thus see considerable changes, and I very much hoped that the new, motivated crew would not have to wait too long for the last containers to leave Syria.

It would take around one and a half months, though, until the last containers had left the country and the force could escort the cargo ships west across the Mediterranean to Italy, where *Ark Futura* transshiped its first-priority cargo to *Cape Ray*. After the hydrolysis process, the by-products were shipped to Germany for destruction. Aside from Germany, the second-priority substances were destroyed in Great Britain, Finland and the US.

I was able to follow this last stage of the operation from back home, where I was responsible for the day-to-day management of the Second Squadron, and I was extremely happy when it was over. Together with a lot of the others who had contributed to this historic mission, I felt that I had contributed to something that really had made the world a safer place. No one could take that feeling away from us.

The following developments in Syria – where the terror organisation Islamic State conquered large swathes of land in 2014 and 2015 – only stressed the importance of the fact that the chemical weapons were now out of reach; because chemical warfare agents in the hands of Islamic State is a scenario no sensible person would want to see.

After calling at Latakia 15 times and picking up a total of 119 containers, Ark Futura *left Syrian territorial waters on 23 June 2014, heading for the Italian port of Gaia Tauro approx. 440 kilometres southeast of Naples. Here the first-priority substances were transferred to* Cape Ray *before* Ark Futura *continued first to Great Britain and then to Finland, where it unloaded the last containers with chemical substances on 21 July.* Taiko, *which simultaneously headed for Finland, had 61 containers on board. Rumour has it that the 700 tons of chemicals in total on board the two ships had a total value of one and a half to two billion kroner. (L.M. Hovtun/Forsvaret.no)*

Operation RECSYR in Retrospect

To me personally, Operation RECSYR constituted the apex of my career. The operation offered me the chance to really use the skills that my – albeit highly operative – varied service in the Danish Defence had given me.

Being able to understand the strategy and the tactics and combining the military needs with the overall strategic foundation was a very interesting challenge, even though my journal makes it clear that it often leaves you very frustrated. You just have to deal with these frustrations if you want the operation to be a success.

This was not an action-packed mission with a lot of kinetic action, but a mission where the leadership was also challenged with ensuring

Esbern Snare *did not return to Denmark until December 2014 after more than 15 months away from Danish waters. An impressive effort by the ship and its two crews. (C. Gustafsen)*

the force was prepared for 'what if' situations. And 'just' waiting for something unpleasant to happen is not always easy. In fact, it is often easier, mentally – though typically also more dangerous – to participate in kinetic warfare, which means that you are engaging the enemy and have a chance to change things. As a leader it is important to be aware of this, as it can be mentally strenuous, even though you do not have bullets flying around your ears.

I have no doubt that the Navy, the Danish Defence and Denmark benefitted from participating in the operation. This has shown that even though we are a small nation, we can do great things at sea, and I have no doubt that we have earned the respect of our partners.

To Bashar al-Assad, Operation RECSYR meant that his forces' capacity for using chemical weapons was reduced. And I have no doubt – because they told me in Latakia – that the pro-Assad military leaders considered the chemical weapons applicable military resources. Of course, they can continue to produce chemical weapons, but the regime will have difficulties using them in the future. This is not to say that everything is well on that front, because it is not. Even while we were removing the chemical substances from the country, there were indications that the military was using chlorine bombs. Because chlorine, unfortunately, is not covered by the convention. So did we do all this hard work only to see them use chlorine bombs? Obviously, this was not the objective. The many tons of chemical weapons we helped destroy can never again be used against innocent civilians, just as they cannot fall into the hands of others who might use them. Therefore, there is no doubt that the operation was a success both tactically and strategically.

Unfortunately, the civil war is still ongoing, but stopping it was not the objective of Operation RECSYR.

As evident from my journal, the regime delayed the last shipments for as long as possible. From the perspective of the regime, this was a sensible tactic, because while we were busy with the shipments, and while the regime was cooperating with us, al-Assad's forces could continue fighting their opponents as no one would risk a situation where the regime no longer wanted to cooperate on removing the chemical substances. So did the operation help Bashar al-Assad? It is hard to say, but we cannot rule out that these very six months enabled him to consolidate his military efforts and relevant cooperation with Russia, among other factors.

In fact, I have become more and more convinced that we may have been a bit naïve with regard to the planned timing. After all, the operation was supposed to last a couple of months only, but it ended up taking around eight months.

The novel aspect of the operation was the diversity through which Denmark contributed to Operation RECSYR. The Danish contribution consisted of personnel from all three services, special forces, the Chemical Emergency Management, the Danish Emergency Management Agency and the Tax Agency. Add to these the Norwegian Coastal Rangers, personnel from Sweden, chemical experts from Finland, personnel from the Norwegian Navy, the British Royal Navy and even a Danish bomb dog, just to mention a few.

A unified effort, where all applicable capacities were used and synchronised toward solving the joint task, a unique and amazing effort.

In the Royal Danish Navy, we have always practised and implemented maritime leadership, recently in connection with the anti-piracy operations, but this time was different because it was a coalition of the willing and capable under Danish leadership, and we have never done such a thing before at this scale. So, yes, the operation set new standards upon which we continue to build today.

As evident from this account of the operation, it was vital to maintain focus on the job and to stick to the plan in order to solve the task. As the reader will have picked up by now, I had to compromise with the more 'rigorous' approach to reports and information via the chain of command on several occasions. You have to be careful when you adopt such an approach, and naturally some may choose to criticise me for this. I do not intend to encourage others to do so or to turn it into standard practice. When you make such choices as a leader, you take a serious risk because you alone are responsible if it fails. Sometimes such an approach is simply necessary in order to meet the overall objective. You must go through the chain of command when asking your home base for something, but sometimes information and requests unfortunately can – because those asking the question are not present in the operational environment – result in uncertainty about the task and the security of those involved. As a military leader, you therefore willingly commit to taking

We made a plan in Moscow and executed it in Syria, and it became clear that the Danish Navy's new, large units, and in this specific situation, the flexible design of the Absalon class, proved extremely well-suited for an operation such as Operation RECSYR. (forsvaret.no)

on the responsibility, also when you fail and you – deliberately – have not informed your home base.

I believe it is evident that this task and its completion very much constituted the highpoint of my career. Being away from my family was hard on me, but it was probably harder on my family, whose everyday life did not change much, and to whom the new conditions and situations I had to face every day were not an issue. On the other hand, when you join the Navy, you know that such hardship is part of being a mariner, and it takes some getting used to, and some just never can.

I do not regret any of the decisions I made during the operation. Could I have done things differently and better? Probably, but not at the time. We all did what we could to make the operation a success, but an undertaking like RECSYR is not a mathematical equation with a fixed result. If I have to think of something I would change today, it would probably be the fact that I did not set an end date for my participation in the operation to begin with, because the uncertainty generated by my open-ended participation, both for my family and for myself, placed unnecessary strain on all of us.

We did what we set out to do, and as far as I am aware everyone was pleased with the outcome of Operation RECSYR – except perhaps the Syrian regime.

The OPCW received the Nobel Peace Prize in 2013 'for its extensive efforts to eliminate chemical weapons' – a prize which I think all the many stout-hearted men and women who participated in Operation RECSYR deserve to be a part of.

Home again, I returned to my job commanding the Second Squadron, thinking that RECSYR had been a 'once in a lifetime' experience, but that is not how things turned out. In the summer of 2016 I once again headed for the Mediterranean – this time as Commander Task Group 1100.10 with a Danish-British force – and Libya on a mission to collect

In the summer of 2016, the Danish Navy repeated the success of Operation RECSYR, when a Danish-led force comprising the support ship Absalon, Ark Futura *and the British* RFA Mounts Bay *collected approx. 500 tons of chemical substances in Libya and transported them to Germany for destruction.*

and facilitate the destruction of the remains of the Libyan chemical weapons programme. Many considered this mission a repetition of Operation RECSYR. This was not the case, however. Operation Removal of Chemical Agents from Libya (RECLIB), as it was called, was very different from RECSYR, one difference being that the presence of the Libyan military in the Libyan port of Misrata was very sporadic. We therefore did not enjoy the same degree of security in port as we had in Latakia. The port of Misrata was famous for its ISIS activity, and unlike Latakia, the port remained open to other ships, cars and individuals, which placed great demands on our emergency readiness. At the same time, the operation was pressed for time, as ISIS was active elsewhere in Libya and we had to get the chemical substances out of the country before the terror organisation had a chance to build enough resources to focus on the area around Misrata. Therefore, Operation RECLIB was tactically more complex and in terms of intelligence more uncertain than RECSYR. Yet it too was a success; the remains of the Libyan chemical weapons programme were eliminated and now cannot be used against Libya's civilian population or for chemical terrorism.

***

Index

References and Suggested Reading

Cramer-Larsen, L. & Jensen, C. (ed.): Borgerkrigen i Syrien. Historisk, politisk, militært. Copenhagen 2014.

Ege, R.T.: "Norske Syria-soldater i bombe-drama" VG, 11 April 2014.

Ege, R.T.: "På innsiden av Norges Syria-oppdrag" VG, 1 December 2015.

Danish Parliament: B 29 Forslag til folketingsbeslutning om dansk bidrag til FN's og OPCW's mission i Syrien. Copenhagen 2013.

Forsvarsavisen. Year 2012-. Accessed on 7 September 2019 at: https://www2.forsvaret.dk/omos/publikationer/forsvarsavisen/Pages/fsv-avisen.aspx

Jensen, M.S.: "Removing Rather Than Cutting Syria's Gordian Knot. Formal and Informal Objectives in the OPCW-UN JOINT MISSION in Syria September 2013 – June 2014" in Odgaard, L. & Silong, S. (ed.), Danish and Chinese Perspectives on the Objectives of United Nations Missions. Copenhagen 2016.

Ludvigsen, P., Pedersen, P.G. & Jørgensen, T.Ø.: "Militær og civile på fælles kurs": Feature, Jyllands-Posten, 7 September 2016.

Mikkelsen, T.: "Fjernelsen af Bashar Assads kemiske våben: Danmark som en lille brik i et stort strategisk puslespil" in Jensen, C. & Vestenskov, D. (ed.), Et farvel til terror? – Krigen mod ISIS 2014. Copenhagen 2015.

Nielsen, S.A.: "Lastet med sennepsgas og kemikalier", Weekendavisen, 23 December 2014.

Nørby, S.: "Denmark's Libya WMD Mission", Warships International Fleet Review, October 2016.

Nørby, S. & Pilgaard, J.: "Doktrinudvikling i Søværnet og oprettelsen af Søværnets Taktiske Stab", Tidsskrift for Søvæsen, 1 February 2017.

Nørby, S. & Wismann, T.: Absalon og Esbern Snare. Søværnets støtteskibe af Absalon-klassen. Helsinge 2016.

OPWC: Report of the OPWC on the implementation of the convention on the prohibition of the development, production, stockpiling and use of chemical weapons and on their destruction in 2013. Tue Hague 2014. Accessed on 7 September at: www.opcw.org/sites/default/files/documents/CSP/C-l9/en/cl904_e_.pdf

Phillips, C.: The Battle for Syria. International Rivalry in the New Middle Bast. Yale 2018.

Poulsen, N.B. & Staun, J. (ed.): Kreml i krig. Ruslands brug af militær magt. Copenhagen 2018.

White House: Statement by the President on the Completion by the M/V Cape Ray of the Destruction of Syria's Declared Chemical Weapons. Office of the Press Secretary, 18 August 2014.

Appendix

Timetable

Date	International level	National level
2010		
18 December	The 'Arab Spring' begins in Tunisia	
2011		
15 March	Riots break out in Syria and subsequently escalate into real civil war	
2013		
21 August	The international community receives first reports of use of toxic gas during hostilities near Damascus	
26 August	The US Government blames President al-Assad's forces for the toxic gas attack on 21 August	
31 August	US President B.H. Obama recommends military attack on President al-Assad's forces in Syria in response to their use of chemical weapons	
11 September	Russia suggests placing Syria's stockpile of chemical agents under international control	
14 September	The Syrian Government adopts the UN Chemical Weapons Convention	
21 September	The Syrian Government provides the OPCW with a list of its stockpiles of chemical weapons	
27 September	The UN Security Council adopts Resolution 2118, demanding the elimination of Syria's chemical weapons	
2 October	The OPCW commences inspection of Syria's chemical facilities	
6 December		*Esbern Snare* makes for Cyprus
19 December		The Danish Parliament adopts Motion B29 on a Danish contribution to the UN-OPCW mission in Syria
27 December	Planning meeting in Moscow	

2014		
6 January		First coordination meeting between Denmark, Norway, Russia and China on board *Esbern Snare*
7 January		First pickup of chemical agents in Latakia
15 January		Change of crew on *Esbern Snare*
15 January		*Montrose* joins the force
27 January		Second pickup
24 February		*Montrose* is relieved by *Diamond*
26 February		Third pickup
28 February		Fourth pickup
3 March		Fifth pickup
5 March		Sixth pickup
9 March		Seventh pickup
14 March		Eighth pickup
18 March	Russia's annexation of the Crimea	
2 April		Change of crew on *Esbern Snare*
10 April		Ninth pickup
16 April		Tenth pickup
19 April		Eleventh pickup
22 April		Twelfth pickup
24 April		Thirteenth pickup
30 April		*Helge Ingstad* is replaced by *Andenes*
15 May		Steen Engelbrecht Pedersen replaces Torben Mikkelsen as commander of the RECSYR force
17 May		*Esbern Snare* is replaced by *Peter Willemoes*
23 June		Last pickup of chemical substances in Latakia
18 August	*Cape Ray* completes destruction of chemical substances	
30 September	Operation RECSYR is considered completed	
2015		
4 January	OPCW declares the destruction of Syria's stockpile of chemical war gasses and the country's ability to produce such substances completed	

Curriculum Vitae for Torben Mikkelsen

Rear Admiral Torben Mikkelsen
Admiral Danish Fleet and Chief of Navy Command

Date and year of birth: 11 March 1963 in Grove, Aulum-Haderup.

Personal life: Married to Kirsten Ryø Mikkelsen. Together the couple have two sons, Nikolaj and Rasmus, born in 1995.

Military education:

1984-87	Royal Danish Naval Academy
1990-92	Junior Staff Course, Royal Danish Defence Academy
1992	Principal Warfare Officers Course
1994	Joint Maritime Course, Portsmouth, United Kingdom
1997	Joint Maritime Command and Staff Course, Halifax, Canada
1998-99	Senior Staff Course, Royal Danish Defence Academy
2005-06	Naval Command Course, Naval War College, Newport, Rhode Island, USA
2006	Defence Resources Management Course, Defence Resources Management Institute, Monterey, California, USA
2007	Senior Workshop on International Rules Governing Military Operations (SWIRMO), International Committee of the Red Cross, Geneva, Switzerland
2012	Chief of Danish Defence – Political security course, Middle East
2012	Combined Force Maritime Component Commander Course, Manama, Bahrain
2013	Chief of Danish Defence – Political security course, Worldwide
2014	Combined Force Maritime Component Commander Course, Naples, Italy
2015	International Symposium Course, College of Defence Studies, National Defence University, Chinese People's Liberation Army, Beijing, People's Republic of China
2017	Generals, Flag Officers and Ambassadors Course 2017-2, NATO Defence College, Rome, Italy

Military career:

1986	Sub-lieutenant
1987	Lieutenant
1992	Lieutenant Commander
1999	Commander
2004	Commander, senior grade
2009	Captain (N)
2015	Commodore
2017	Rear Admiral

Military assignments:

1982-83	Conscript, Zealand Life Regiment (mechanized infantry)
1987-89	Corvettes, Navigation-, Deck-, and Communication Officer
1989-90	Minelayer N83 *Sjælland*, Communication Officer
1992-93	Patrol Vessel P554 *Makrelen*, Executive Officer
1993-94	Corvette F356 *Peter Tordenskiold*, Principal Warfare Officer
1994-95	Corvette F356 *Peter Tordenskiold*, Operations Officer
1995-98	Patrol Vessel P552 *Havkatten* (ASW), Commanding Officer
1999-01	Defence Command Denmark, Personnel Branch, Staff Officer
2001-02	Danish Task Group, Staff Operations Officer
2002-03	Danish Task Group, Chief of Staff
2003-04	Corvette F356 *Peter Tordenskiold*, Commanding Officer
2004-05	Corvette F356 *Peter Tordenskiold*, Commanding Officer, Division (21) Commander
2006-08	Defence Command Denmark, J3 Branch Head
2008-09	Defence Command Denmark, J32 Branch Head, Operations- and Intelligence Centre
2009-10	Admiral Danish Fleet Headquarters, Assistant Chief of Staff, Operations and Logistics
2010-13	Defence Command Denmark, Executive Office for Chief of Defence
2013-15	Commander 2nd Squadron (Dec. 2013 – May 2014 Commander Task Group 420.01 Operation Removal of Chemical Agents from Syria)
2015-17	Commander, Danish Task Group
2017-19	Chief of Naval Staff, Joint Defence Command
2019-	Admiral Danish Fleet, Royal Danish Navy Command

International operations:

1994 Operation SHARP GUARD, Former Yugoslavia

2004 Operation ACTIVE ENDEVAOUR.

2013-14 Operation RECSYR, Commander Task Group 420.01.

2016 Operation RECLIB, Commander Task Group 1100.10.

Decorations:

Commander of the Order of Dannebrog

Badge of Honour for Good Service in the Navy, 25 years

Badge of Honour Danish Emergency Management Agency

Badge of Honour Danish Home Guard

Medal for International Operations, 1948-2009

Medal for International Operations, Operation RECSYR

Medal for International Operations, Operation RECLIB

French Order: Commandeur de l'Ordre du Mérite Maritime

Polish Order for Spirit of Self-sacrifice and Courage

NATO Medal, Operation SHARP GUARD (NATO-FY)

B 29 Motion for Parliamentary Resolution on Danish Contribution to the UN and OPCW Mission in Syria

By: Rasmus Helveg Petersen (RV)
Committee: Defence Committee
Session: 2013-14
Status: Passed

About the motion for resolution
Administrative process:

- Presented on 06-12-2013
- Processed/referred to committee on 10-12-2013
- Report published on 18-12-2013
- Processed/passed on 19-12-2013

Ministerial Area: Ministry of Foreign Affairs of Denmark
Summary: With this parliamentary resolution, the Danish Parliament assents to Denmark's contribution to the UN-OPCW mission in Syria with a view to securing the elimination of the Syrian chemical weapons programme within the framework of the UN Security Council resolution 2118 of 27 September 2013. The UN would like Denmark to contribute with maritime transport, maritime escort and maritime command capacities, including managing the overall maritime transport operation. In addition, formal requests have been received from the UN of a Danish contribution to the joint UN-OPCW mission in the form of a personal protection team as well as air transport capacity.

The maritime contribution will consist of two cargo ships, a flexible support ship of the Absalon class for security escort and a maritime command team. The contribution is expected to consist of up to 30 individuals (transport), 200 individuals (escort) and 20 individuals (command team), though the final number will i.a. depend on other nations' contribution to the operation. Maritime special forces will form part of the escort contribution and may be present on the cargo ships. The air transport contribution will consist of a C-130J transport aircraft. The contribution shall be ready to deploy to Cyprus to contribute to mission within 96 hours. The contribution will consist of up to 25 individuals.

In addition, Denmark will support the UN's employment of a personal protection team to support the joint UN-OPCW mission. The personal protection team will consist of up 19 specially trained soldiers. The personal protection team will be tasked with protecting the special coordinator of the mission and other senior personnel.

Voting: Passed 97 in favour (V, S, RV, SF, EL, LA, KF, UFG) 14 against (DF) 0 neither in favour nor against the motion.

Esbern Snare

Technical data

Overall dimensions
Length overall: 137.6 m
Max width: 19.5 m
Max draught below sonar dome: 6.3 m
Max draught below propellers: 6.1 m
Max draught hull: 5.3 m
Max height above basic front mast: 31.3 m
Max displacement: 6,653 t
Max dead weight: 2,412 t
Design draught hull: 4.65 m
Dead weight at draught of 4.65 m: 1,230 t

Capacities
Fuel oil: 855 m^3 (up to 910 m^3, if retention tanks are included)
Helicopter fuel oil: 150 m^3
Ballast tanks: 939 m^3
Lubrication oil: 33 m^3
Freshwater: 142 m^3
Flex deck: 902 m^2
Tonnage: 1,700 t

Propulsion power: 2 x 8,200 kW/22,000 hp
Max speed at draught of 4.65 m: 25 knots
Operating speed at 90 % engine power and dead weight of 1,700 t: 23 knots
Range: 9,000 nautical miles (approx. 16,600 km) at 15 knots
Endurance without replenishment: 28 days
Crew: originally 99, today 113 (with room for another 200 individuals)
Helicopters: 2
Response vessels: 2 SRC 90E

Armament
Harpoon anti-ship missiles
Sea Sparrow anti-aircraft missiles
1 x 127-mm Mk 45 autocannon
2 x 35-mm Millennium revolver cannons (CIWS)
2 x 2-MU-90 anti-submarine torpedoes
8 x 50-caliber (12.7 mm) TMGs
2 x 37-mm salute cannons

Other data
Hull number: L17 (Changed to F342 in 2020)
International call sign: OUFB
Shipyard: Odense Staalskibsværft A/S (Construction number 192)
Classification: Det Norske Veritas Naval + 1A1 NAVAL (dnk)
ICE-C, HELDK, E0, ICS, NBC-2, NV
Squadron: 2nd Squadron, Frederikshavn

Helge Ingstad

Technical data

Overall dimensions
Length overall: 134 m
Max width: 16.8 m
Max draught: 7.6 m
Max displacement: 5,290 t

Capacities
Top speed: 26 knots

Range: 4,500 nautical miles (approx. 8,300 km)
Crew: 120 (with room for another 26 individuals)
Helicopters: 1 NH90

Armament
8 x Naval Strike anti-ship Missiles (NSM)
32 x Evolved SeaSparrow anti-aircraft missiles
1 x 76-mm Melara Super Rapid autocannon
Depth charges
2 x 2-Sting Ray torpedoes
4 x 50-caliber (12.7 mm) TMGs
Other data
Classification: Fridtjof Nansen
Hull number: F313
Shipyard: Navantia, Ferrol, Spain

Ark Futura

Technical data
Type: RO-RO Cargo Ship

Overall dimensions
Length overall: 183.1 m
Max width: 25.23 m
Max draught: 7.35 m
Displacement: 18,725 t
Top speed: 18.5 knots
Crew: 18

Shipyard: Cantiere Navale «Visentini» di Visentini Francesco & C, Donada, Italy
Completed: 7 April 1995
Launched: 13 October 1995
Delivered: 4 June 1996

Taiko

Technical data
Type: RO-RO Cargo Ship

Overall dimensions
Length overall: 262.3 m
Max width: 32.26 m
Max draught: 11.73 m
Displacement: 29,900 t
Top speed: 21 knots
Crew: 25

Shipyard: Hyundai Heavy Industries, Ulsan, South Korea
Launched: February 1984.